One Step at A Time

A Remarkable Journey
of Obedience to the
Will of God

Donald William Benner

LifeSource Publishing
Crown Point, Indiana

One Step At A Time

Copyright 2000 ©
Donald W. Benner

Cover design by Michael J. Rigg

All rights reserved. This book is protected under the copyright laws of the United States of America. No part of this book may be reproduced, stored in a retrieval system, or transmitted in any form or by any means, electronic, mechanical, photocopying, recording or otherwise, without the prior written permission of the publisher and copyright owners. The only exception is for brief excerpts to be used for a book review.

ISBN: 0-9675987-4-5

Library of Congress Catalog Card Number
00-107099

All Scripture quotations, unless otherwise indicated, are taken from the Holy Bible, New International Version.

Printed in the USA

LifeSource PUBLISHING

P.O. Box 471, Crown Point, Indiana, 46307
219-661-0524
www.lifesourcepublishing.com

Dedication

I dedicate this book to my wife, Rose Ann, who also wanted to write it, but didn't have the time, because she was always too occupied with the Lord's work. We have been inseparable throughout our marriage, and our missionary adventure, and we are looking forward to leaving together in the rapture.

Prologue

Many exciting and some morbid things happened to us in our many years of missionary service. Most of them made interesting stories to tell in churches or in Sunday school classes during our visits to the United States.

Jack and Laura Martin always invited us to their lovely home whenever we were in the Denver area. They would also invite friends over to share the fellowship and delicious food, and then egg us on to tell something that happened in our ministry that might be of interest to their friends.

On one such evening, while we were gathered in their cozy family room, we seemed to be especially inspired and rattled off a number of incidents, and Jack said, "You guys ought to write a book". That is what led to this publication. It is a narrative of our miraculous spiritual experiences, some of our not so spiritual experiences, and some of our mistakes.

This book was written for the following reasons:

1. **To inspire older people to give their remaining productive years to service on the mission field.** I was a 52 year-old successful businessman, motivated by money, when I left a lucrative position I had held for 20 years, and went to Central America to start a whole new career, motivated by a desire to serve. I gave my life to the Lord just 4 years before that.

2. To testify to so-called "unfit" missionary candidates that God has a work for them to do, just as they are. My inclination, when I first felt a call to go to the mission field, was to subdue my desire to go because of feeling inadequate. I had no Bible school degree, no experience as a pastor, no training in cross-cultural living, and no idea of what I would do as a missionary. But sort of like Abraham, "Who ... obeyed and went, even though he did not know where he was going." (Heb. 11:8), I went to language school in Costa Rica, trusting God to find a place for me. And He did.

3. To prove to missions-minded people that they can go, even if they have to go as an independent missionary. We don't recommend this, but if you are sure you have a definite call from God, you should proceed and obey on faith. He will provide the place, the support, and the success if you are moving in the Spirit. We wrote to dozens of mission agencies and no one wanted us. We went on our own as self-supporting volunteers. God has been faithful for all these years, and we expect Him to be the same tomorrow that He is now, and was in the past. (Heb. 13:8)

It is my prayer that those who are hesitant to obey God's call to service, for whatever reason, will read this book and be encouraged to trust Him with their future. It will be worth it.

Donald W. Benner

TABLE OF CONTENTS

	Prologue	
One	Receiving A Call	1
Two	The Miracle Way To Missions	23
Three	Why El Salvador	35
Four	Saved For Witnessing	47
Five	Foreign Missionary Work Begins	55
Six	Getting Started In El Salvador	65
Seven	We Serve A Miracle Working God	91
Eight	Fraught With Frauds	107
Nine	Changed Lives	139
	What About The Future?	

1

Receiving A Call

I held my mother's hand tightly as the big iron gates swung open. We walked through them into a different world. At six years of age, I screamed and kicked when I heard my Mom tell the admissions director of the institution that I was to be left there while she returned home to Berwick, Pennsylvania without me. Knowing my vulnerability was animals, she knelt down to get eye level with me, took me by both arms, and promised, "Donny, don't cry. They'll give you your own pony to ride and take care of." Magically I calmed down and was led away.

After many hours, mother walked back out the huge, highly decorated gates alone, leaving me with complete strangers. That fateful day started a new chapter in my young life. I was a frightened, confused, and sad six-year-old little boy.

My father died of a heart attack at 24; I was five. My mother took in laundry and baked bread, cookies and cakes to sell around the little town of Berwick, trying to care for my older brother, younger sister and me. Dad left no insurance, and in 1929 there was the Great

Depression that mother had to contend with. Pennsylvania had no help for widows or their children in those miserable days.

The odds finally overcame my mother's efforts to keep her family together. Her health faltered due to overwork and stress. She caved in, and reluctantly turned my brother and sister over to an evangelical orphanage in Lewisburg, Pennsylvania. Eventually my sister went to a strict Christian foster home in Bloomsburg, while I was deposited unceremoniously in the orphanage I mentioned earlier. We were never to be a close family again.

I don't know how many times I asked my governess when I'd get my pony, only to be ridiculed. I realized my trust in mother was broken: I felt betrayed.

I reluctantly attended the required chapel services every day, and twice on Sundays. The services were conducted somewhat like a children's library story hour. Despite interesting readings from books or magazines like Reader's Digest and lectures from returning, successful alumni that extolled the advantages of being raised in the orphanage, I heard readings from the Bible also. "My Word will not return void," says the Scriptures, and it's true! After I gave my heart to the Lord 41 years later, I recalled many of those often-read verses that were interspersed with the stories.

Banker Steven Girard founded the orphanage in the 1800s. Mr. Girard willed a major part of his vast wealth for educating poor orphans who had lost at least their fathers, and as I grew up there, I appreciated more and more what he had done for me: good clothes, the best medical attention, a superior education, high moral values; and all free. I excelled on the varsity swimming and debating teams and graduated from Girard High School in 1941.

After graduating from Girard High School with an excellent education, I went to Dearborn, Michigan to work for the Ford Motor Company where I became a purchasing agent. At nineteen I married a young southern girl right out of high school. We had five beautiful children, one of whom died very young. The mother of our four remaining children died. These children are all very successful and I am very proud of them.

My lovely wife, Rose Ann Murphy, on the other hand, grew up in a home full of love and family values. She had a bout with cancer on her leg when she was ten years old, and was hit by a car that then fractured the other leg when she was 12. She was in a coma several days and had a concussion and a broken pelvis. In each case, the love and care given by her sweet parents and older sister, she claims, had as much healing power as the severe treatments.

She gave her heart to the Lord when she was 19, and subsequently helped win the rest of her family to Him. In those days she was engaged to a handsome Catholic young man, and was taking instructions at his church preparing to join his denomination. Rose Ann felt uneasy about this and one day, while sitting alone in a huge, cathedral-like, dark Catholic Church, she heard the Lord speak to her, saying: I want you to worship Me the way I want to be worshipped." As she was meditating, the image of Calvary Temple's building in Denver, Colorado appeared in her mind. Soon she attended Calvary Temple and immediately felt comfortable and knew she was where God wanted her to be.

Being greatly interested in music, she joined the large choir. She professed being a Christian and truly believed she was. Then one Sunday, the Holy Spirit convicted her of her need to accept Christ as her Savior. She left the choir loft to kneel at the altar, and tearfully but joyfully gave her heart and life to God. For a robed singer to conspicuously leave the choir from behind the platform, and make her way to the altar in front of the platform, sobbing before everyone, was unusual, and took courage.

Not long after that Rose Ann felt a call to be a missionary. To receive a missionary appointment she was required to graduate from a Bible school, pastor in a church for at least three years, and be ordained, among other things. Her family was very poor, but she applied to Bethany Bible College in Santa Cruz, California, and prayerfully worked her way through their curriculum until she graduated with a degree in Christian Education.

She was permitted to go to Central America for four years as a single Assemblies of God missionary under special appointment, where she was known as Sister Murphy. She worked with children in El Salvador and in Costa Rica, she also went to the same language school I eventually went to, to learn Spanish.

Her heart's desire was to attain full appointment as a missionary, so she returned to Colorado to pastor and seek her ordination. She served as the pastor for a while in a Spanish-speaking church in a town called Center in Colorado. The Center church did well under her guidance and then she was finally ordained in a beautiful service at which the venerable preacher on the Revival Time Radio Program, the late C. M. Ward, gave a memorable message.

During this time I became a successful businessman. I had been elected president of the Denver Chapter of the Full Gospel Business Men's Fellowship International (FGBMFI). We had early Wednesday morning prayer meetings followed by breakfast at which all chapter members were invited. Many times someone who had visited Rose Ann's church in Center the previous Sunday, requested prayer for Sister Murphy. Through these numerous prayer requests over many months, I felt I had begun to know her well by reputation.

I finally got to meet the "famous" Sister Murphy at one of our chapter breakfasts. I was smitten immediately and we began to date. After much prayer and searching for God's will, we decided to get married, and that changed her plans of immediately returning to Central America as a missionary. Though neither of us knew it at the time, in just a few years we would be on our way to Central America as missionaries. Our huge wedding, attended by 320 friends, was officiated by our pastor, Dr. Charles Blair, in Calvary Temple where we both found Christ. In that church we later would also be commissioned for the mission field.

Hunger takes different forms; ours was to know more of God's Word, and to know Christ better. That's why we eventually sold our extravagant house in the exclusive Cherry Hills section of Suburban Denver, and bought one close to our church, Calvary Temple, directly behind our pastor's home. This was in Denver's upscale Polo Club area, an exclusive residential neighborhood located in the city limits.

We loved our ample-sized, ranch style house with its quiet patio in the back where many charcoal fires cooked up some of the best barbecues. We would sit on our large front porch on Sunday afternoons and visit with friends and watch an occasional car pass by. (These days the street has a lot of traffic.) In front we put in a circle driveway and we planted a lot of trees and beautiful flowers. At that time we hoped we'd live there the rest of our lives. It was a smaller home than the one we left in Cherry Hills, but we enjoyed it more. That was one of the reasons we thought it would be our permanent home. Another was, we could easily walk to church whenever the doors opened, and visit with our pastor and his family over the back fence.

What a good life I had! God was so good; I had an enviable job with high income and an open expense account, company Cadillac, worldwide travel that permitted visits to missionaries while on a business trip, and a wonderful family.

Then one balmy Sunday night, we went to a service at Calvary Temple that threatened to put a crack in our earthly bliss. Veteran missionary statesman Paul Kaufman, who served in China, gave a challenging message about the need for all kinds of workers to go to the mission field. He spoke of the many skills needed there more than preachers. He impressed on us that though we usually tell God about <u>our</u> needs, God also had a need and we, and only we humans, could meet <u>His</u> need. He needs people!

Paul Kaufman got close to my career experience when he mentioned that even a businessman would be extremely useful in missions. The service ended with an invitation for those who were interested in giving their lives to missions, trusting God to show them how He could use them, to step to the altar as a sign of such a commitment. While my eyes were closed and I was in an attitude of prayer, I felt the Holy Spirit wooing me to respond. When I realized that my wife had moved toward the aisle, I filed close behind her. We knelt at the altar together to surrender our lives to God for use in missions.

Paul's text was Luke chapter 5, verses 1 through 11. He pointed out how missionaries who were fishing for souls in countries where Jesus told them to go, were experiencing revivals that were "filling their nets" with a great harvest of believers, and they needed help to disciple them.

Along with about 20 others who joined us at the altar, we were herded into a counseling room where we could ask questions of veteran missionary statesman Gene Martin, missionary Paul Kaufman and missions minded pastor Charles Blair. (Pastor Blair always judged the success of Calvary Temple not by how many seats he could fill; but by how many he could empty by sending people to mission fields). Thinking back, I had no idea where that step of faith we made that night would lead us. We sincerely made ourselves available for missionary work, if God wanted to use us for such service.

Tucked away in my heart, as part of my commitment, was one important reservation I secretly made with God; I did not want to go where it would be necessary to learn another language. I was older than most people who go to the mission field, and I didn't want to "waste" a lot of possible missionary time sitting in classrooms. I didn't relish the idea of going to school at my age either. Just over half of a century had slipped by since my mother birthed me in Pennsylvania.

Our blissful home, as well as our cars and other perks, gradually began to seem less important after that commitment. We realized that we could only enjoy the material after it became immaterial. "Things of earth grew strangely dim", as the hymn goes, in the light of our possible service to God in a different world. My job, especially, began to seem like a waste of time as my ambitions and goals had changed. Although others envied me for my world travel, company cars, expense account, authority and good income, I began to lose interest in these benefits also. I used to know the price of everything, and the value of nothing. Truly, my values, priorities and desires were changing as God prepared me for the plan he had for my life.

Guilt, combined with the Holy Spirit's calling, can be a powerful motivator. Looking back, I can see that part of my desire to become a missionary was caused by a guilty feeling over having passed the halfway point of my life long before I accepted Christ. I had a lot of wasted time to redeem for Him during my remaining years.

Another impulse to do missionary work stemmed from a guilty feeling I had over my excessive lifestyle. I heard many missionaries' stories that challenged me to get out of my comfort zone and do something for Christ among less fortunate people. As someone aptly put it,

" I wanted to go some place awful to do something meaningful".

Another guilt trip was created by thoughts of how much Jesus did for me, and how little I did for Him. I owed Him. Of course, the call He gave me to be available for missionary work was the strongest motivator of all.

Before giving my heart to the Lord, I lived beyond my means because I earned a lot of money and felt secure economically. The more I earned, the more I spent. Now that I've had the experience of living on faith in a developing country, I have great pangs of regret. Many times I wish I had invested my money in income-producing ventures instead of income-consuming junk with no eternal value. I would have had the funds needed to be comfortably self-supporting. I ended up in a country where 70 percent of the people earn less than a U.S. paperboy. I see there's a way people can live happily without all the things which we think we need to live with in the United States. It's a constant reminder of my foolishness in past years.

I confirmed by my own experience that you reap what you sow. For more than twenty years I sowed selfishness, foolishness, and pride while building a career - then I reaped the loss of all my income.

By investing my retirement fund in a loan guaranteed by a personal note, I thought I had enough income to support my family on the mission field—until that investment soured, and eventually lost it. The lesson I learned was not to trust in a retirement fund or in other securities, but to trust in God alone. However, by the time our investment failed, God had begun to impress on people and churches to support our ministry. God is faithful. I believe He helped us survive because we had tithed to our church for years, and had also given offerings to help many missionaries before becoming missionaries ourselves. I am also convinced that because we answered His call for service, He provided what we needed to be able to stay where He put us. God always provides for our daily needs and often even our wants.

I was very fortunate to have experienced for many years a measure of luxurious living, and then a time of having almost nothing. When we finally lost our retirement fund after 18 years on the field, we didn't feel devastated because we were so busy doing what we were called to do. We went from being relatively well off to practically nothing to eat, at one time, and had no regrets. In fact, we learned a lot from this experience.

But I am ahead of my story. After we committed to being missionaries, we applied to all the mission agencies whose addresses we could find, to no avail. No one wanted us. I was beginning to think that our call to the mission field was our own impetuous desire, and not God's idea.

I had planned on resigning my job when we received a mission board appointment. But one day in 1976, while I was home recovering from a very serious operation, my colleagues on our company's board of directors sent two halting, embarrassed emissaries to tell me they wanted to make a change in my position - they wanted to give it to someone else. The two fellow officers were visibly shaken when my wife and I both exclaimed, "Praise the Lord" in unison. They were expecting an argument and a battle, but instead they received full cooperation. We sensed God at work. You see, I had a lucrative job with lots of perks; it was hard to give it up for any reason. I wasn't obeying God in His leading so he had to push me in His direction. Sometimes the push can be a shove that might not be so gentle. God had to intervene and bring about His will in our lives. We explained that to my two flabbergasted "friends", and they didn't know what to think. We made plans right then and there to leave the company as quickly as possible on an early retirement.

The industry our company served is a rather narrow one, and word got around quickly that I was resigning. I enjoyed a good reputation among my peers as a mover and shaker in the marketing of the products we manufactured. When I joined the company as marketing vice-president in 1957, it was on the ropes financially. I had been their representative in Detroit, where we sold over 50% of their total worldwide sales. I persuaded management to let me go to Denver to try to turn it around before they declared bankruptcy. Starting with sales of $150,000, in five years we were selling over a million dollars a year, and sales were climbing exponentially. When I left the company sales were $12 million a year.

That's why former competitors contacted me about going to work for them. It was heady stuff. I almost forgot about moving somewhere else for the Lord. Especially when a German manufacturer sent an envoy to Denver to tell me that they had long wanted to break into the American market, and they felt that I could make it happen.

While they were thinking that way, I was thinking about how happy God was going to be when I started a Christian factory, put in a chapel, hired believers, and developed a moral marketing method free of alcohol and other so-called sales stimulants. Surely He would bless such an operation with outstanding success, and my new company would outshine my former company.

The well-financed Germans agreed to my terms: they would put up the necessary funds to build, rent or buy, and equip a factory to be located in Denver (so we wouldn't have to give up our beautiful house), and they would give me 50% of the stock in a newly-formed American corporation, of which I was to be the president and chief executive officer.

I immediately began to form a plan of action. I looked for a factory; developed detailed one-year and five-year budgets with projected costs and sales, and contacted some winners in other companies, who were Christians, to come on board. After months of long hours of work and much preparation, the Lord showed me that this was the very thing I was so anxious to leave in my former employment: long hours, intensive work and responsibility, many days away from home and church, and striving to make money and more money. What a dumb goal! But I was like a Dalmatian from a firehouse that jumped on the fire engine every time a fire alarm sounded. "Business" was my business for such a long time that I was tempted to accept the new marketing challenge.

That was when I asked the Lord to close the door on this position and open another if He didn't like the idea. To help this process, I wrote the surprised Germans that I was a born-again Christian, would not provide alcohol at sales or other marketing meetings, and would designate space for a chapel in our factory. That did it! The German management decided they didn't want to partner with a religious fanatic and I didn't want to be unequally yoked, so our relationship was called off. That door was closed. This ambitious fleshly-conceived plan was obviously not the mission field to which God had called me.

We went back to the drawing board; in other words, the prayer room. Where would we go? What would we do? How could we do it? Then we got another humanly inspired idea: we would go to Costa Rica, where my wife once lived. She loved it there and I would evangelize in the large colony of English-speaking retired Americans. Rose Ann would work in the Spanish-speaking community, especially with children. She would use her gift of working with the kids using her fluent Spanish. With this plan, I would not need to learn another language. We would be self-supporting because we would buy a tourist gift shop or something else in Costa Rica, to provide the income we needed to live in the "Gardens of Central America". Of course, I wouldn't be "suffering much for Jesus", either. In retrospect, it sounds like I was looking for a semi-retired lifestyle instead of a mission field.

We thought this was another wonderful plan, and excitedly talked it over with some old-time missionaries serving in Costa Rica whom we had been supporting. They wisely advised us to go there first and "test the waters" because things had changed drastically since Rose Ann lived there six years before.

We had also been supporting other missionaries in El Salvador and Panama. We decided that since they were near Costa Rica, it would be a good opportunity to see their work, and sense whether or not God wanted us to serve in one of those countries. We especially wanted to look around in Costa Rica to get the feel of what we thought was a good plan. We were sure the Lord couldn't wait for us to move there and implement it.

In El Salvador, we stayed with a wonderful, dedicated missionary family who always treated visitors like good relatives. They took us everywhere we wanted to go, and to places they wanted us to see. Little did we know then what a big part that family would play in our future.

We went to see a heart-breaking sight: a sea of tin and cardboard shacks, thrown up on a hill formed by garbage and junk piled up over many years, when it was a city dump. The missionaries appropriately named it Mount Trashmore. The people living there picked through the trash for something they could eat, use, or sell. Their shacks were mostly made of the junk they gleaned from their surroundings.

The squatters had no water, electricity or toilets in their shacks, called "champitas" in Spanish. We learned that 70% of the people in El Salvador lived this way. The missionaries had started a school and church called "Milagro (Miracle)", at the base of Mt. Trashmore, to serve that poor community.

It is interesting to note that in a couple of years we would be back at the Milagro School and Church, holding weekly chapel services in the adjoining Milagro

Church for the school students. I would be establishing a kitchen for a new program initiated for feeding the children during school lunch hours. It was for this program that David Wilkerson, author of *The Cross and the Switchblade*, supplied the finances.

I met a child on a dirt path between the champitas, with his fist clenched so tight he couldn't take the friendly hand I offered to him. But the temptation to shake hands with a North American was so great that he finally released the big cockroach he was holding and with frustration grabbed my extended hand. I couldn't hide my shock and disgust at the thought of him carrying a cockroach around and offering that hand for me to shake. The missionary asked him in Spanish why he was carrying it, and his reply almost turned my stomach sick. He was taking it home to use in the soup for something to eat.

We saw another school our host had established so poor children could get an education. When he started it many years before our visit, it was hard to find Christian teachers. John, who is a Pentecostal missionary, begged two bi-lingual Baptist missionaries to teach, and they finally agreed— on one condition— that they have nothing to do with speaking in tongues. John was desperate for good teachers, so he accepted the terms.

One day, the children were being led in a devotional before school started, when several of them began to praise God in perfect English. The teachers listened with amazement, which turned to shock when they realized that the children hadn't learned a word of English, but were worshipping in a tongue inspired by the Holy Spirit. Of course, thereafter, they eliminated their original reservation for teaching there, and became comfortable with glossolalia and other spiritual gifts. The more time we spent with all the missionaries in El Salvador, the more we began to feel God calling us there instead of Costa Rica.

Just before we left for San Jose, Costa Rica we attended a high school graduation party for the daughter of a missionary couple. I was sitting on the breezy patio of their home in the damp night air. I had very little sleep the past few nights, and I developed a severe case of tropical flu. It hit me hard the following day as we were flying to San Jose.

Suffering terribly from the flu as we arrived, nothing about Costa Rica looked inviting. The cramped little room we stayed in at a second-class downtown hotel became a virtual prison because of the torrential rains outside. All of the missionaries we knew were tied up with their own programs, so we took buses to see the places where Rose Ann lived and worked as a single missionary years before. The buses in San Jose were infested with fleas. I found I was allergic to them. With the flu, the dreary rainy weather, itchy welts all along my belt line, and the virtual confinement in the little hotel room, I was miserable.

Rose Ann found that the country had indeed changed a lot since she left it many years before. Everything was much more expensive, and gift shops and souvenir stores abounded everywhere. The intense competition meant meager profits, so that such a business was unlikely to provide sufficient income for our family. Our plan to serve in Costa Rica began to unravel.

After three tortuous days, I confessed to Rose Ann that I did not agree with her previous assessment that Costa Rica was like a paradise. I hated it, and announced that we were packing up and returning to the United States on the next possible flight.

"We're wasting time and money," I told Rose Ann. "Let's get back to Denver and find something to do there." I disliked Costa Rica in particular and Central America in general. I could see my misguided plan of being a missionary in that country was not as pleasing to the Lord as I thought it would be.

It was on that fact-finding trip, (when we were trying to learn of God's will for us) that I discovered that here is a place where I was unhappy. I was eager to return home to Denver. Rose Ann felt that the Lord put it in her mind to go to the missionary language school while we were still in Costa Rica, to take a test so her former Spanish language studies could be added to her college credits. "I might want to teach Spanish someday," she told me.

The next day we took a taxi in a downpour of rain to the old colonial building that was the missionary language school where Rose Ann had arranged to take the test. I didn't want to board any more flea-infested buses, and to avoid the torrential rain; a taxi ride was the best option.

The school hadn't changed a bit, she observed. All the classrooms in the old, creaky wooden building were empty because the students were on a trimester break. It was around July 8 or 10, 1976, and only the young teacher, who was going to give the test, welcomed us. He ushered me into one of the damp, high-ceilinged old classrooms, and led Rose Ann off in another direction. He said the test would take two hours and suggested I make myself comfortable, or come back later. I sat at a wobbly student desk and felt chilled by the dampness that penetrated the old walls. From my jacket pocket, I pulled out a book I planned on reading during the flight back to Denver, written about a famous embezzler and "con man" named Robert Vesco, who was living in exile in Costa Rica at the time. I bought the book at a bookstore in San Jose because I visited Robert several times in his New Jersey office when I was in business, and was fascinated by him. He could have conned me any day.

I pulled my jacket collar tight around my neck and started to read. I don't know how long I read nor how far into the book I got, when something miraculous and wonderful happened.

The classroom was suddenly engulfed in a brilliant light, and I dropped the book. I was stunned. As I looked around the room, I could only see light, but all the while I was feeling God's presence. "My son," an audible voice said through the brightest part of the light, "I want you to learn the Spanish language because I have a work for you to do among the Spanish-speaking people."

As suddenly as it came, the beautiful light melted from the room and the message repeated in my mind two or three times, as if to be sure I wouldn't forget it. I don't know if a tape recorder would have been able to record that voice but it was just as real and audible as my own.

As I sat there meditating on what had happened, and forgetting I had specified that I didn't want to learn another language, I heard the heavy steps of a man echoing in the hall. The man came down the hall and entered the room opposite the classroom I was in. I knew that was the office for the language school. The timing of his appearance was perfect. I couldn't wait to be obedient to the message I had so miraculously been given. I walked into the office and found the director, Dr. Kobel, seated at his desk.

"Sir," I began, after introducing myself, "God spoke to me about learning Spanish."

"That's wonderful, " he replied, but seemed unimpressed. "Almost everyone who comes here says the same thing because this is a language school for missionaries."

"But it's true," I countered. "God just spoke to me across the hall, so I'd like to register for a course in your school."

"What mission board are you with?" he asked as he continued to move papers around on his desk.

"None", I said, "but God called me to be a missionary.

"You have to be a missionary sent by a board to study here, and you have to register in advance. I can't accept you. Besides, we have a 3-year waiting list, so it wouldn't be possible to enroll you now," Dr. Kobel declared as he shuffled papers on his desk.

"But my experience happened across the hall just before you walked into the building. I heard a voice say that I was to learn Spanish. Why would God tell me that here if this isn't the place where I'm supposed to learn it?"

"I don't know," he said, "but you could come here in several years if you registered today, and if you got an appointment as a missionary."

"I sure don't understand why God told me to learn Spanish while I am visiting your school, and you can't take me," I explained.

"Just a minute," Dr. Kobel said. "This is strange. Here in today's mail is a cancellation, and it's too late to get another student here by opening day on August 28. Can you be here, ready to study by that date?" (That happened on July 11, 1976).

Impetuously, I assured him I would. I didn't even think about all I'd have to do in the next 48 days, 13 of which were days we would use just for driving to Costa Rica. I just knew God was at work, and a good work He starts, He finishes.

About then Rose Ann appeared in the hall, where I met her enthusiastically.

"Guess what?" I announced. "We're moving to Costa Rica!"

"When?" she asked, her face expressing disbelief.

"Right away." Her changed expression implied that she thought that I was kidding.

"I thought you hated it here," she said.

"Not anymore." I explained. "I think this is a wonderful place, and I've registered to learn Spanish here. We've got to get back to Denver right away so that we can pack up and return here by August 28th!" The next day we were on an airplane heading back to the United States to begin an exciting, miracle-laden adventure.

On the airplane trip home, I began to make a list of things we had to do, and the approximate time it would take, allowing 13 days for the overland trip by car back to Costa Rica. The more things I listed, the more it seemed impossible apart from more miracles from God. The list started with "Sell house," followed by "sell furniture, sell car, invest money, buy appropriate car for the trip, get papers to take dogs, passports for the children, find a mission board, get visas for each country, get maps and routing through U.S., Mexico, Guatemala, El Salvador, Honduras, Nicaragua, and Costa Rica, arrange finances for trip, etc." All this had to be done in 35 days.

When it's God's will, He makes the way, or as we say in El Salvador, "If God tells you to go, He'll provide the horse." That doesn't mean that everything will necessarily go easy, for the devil will interfere and try to prevent the accomplishment of God's will. But we learned that no matter what happens, if you do what God clearly wants you to do, you would succeed. To make it there on time we would certainly need miracles, <u>and we got them</u>!

2

THE MIRACLE WAY TO MISSIONS

The first week after returning from Central America, I had some spiritual battles to face. The devil bombarded me with various accusations, trying to replace my faith with fear and discouragement. Even after having such a vivid, mountaintop experience in Costa Rica, where the Lord spoke to me just days before, I began to have doubts. "Who was I that God would speak to me?" When God parted the Red Sea and permitted the Israelites to cross over on dry ground, they soon murmured against Him. They doubted He would lead them to a new land. I was no stronger spiritually than they were. The devil was saying, "You can't" and God was saying, "You can."

The enemy whispered things like, "You know you're a very impetuous man. This whole idea of going to Central America is your own." Then again I heard, "You'll burn all your bridges here, and you'll get down there where you'll have no credit, your income will dry up, and there won't be anything you can do to keep yourself busy. You're not a preacher, not even a missionary. What can you do?" I even heard satan say, "God didn't say He'd take care of you, did He? He just said He wanted you to learn Spanish. You know you can't learn it. Besides, you told God you didn't want to learn another language. You shouldn't go."

Finally, I got the victory. The rebuttal came from God, early one morning when I was praying and reading God's Word. As I read in Genesis Chapter 28, a verse lit up like a neon sign. I was attracted to it in a supernatural way. I knew it was God's reassurance to forge ahead with His plans. Verse 15 said; "Go for it!" at least that's the way I read it:

"I am with you and will watch over you wherever you go, and I will bring you back to this land. I will not leave you, until I have done what I have promised you." Gen. 28:15 (NIV)

To me this was another miracle. What assurance God gave me. He would be with me, and protect me. Since the verse said He would bring me back to my country, it meant I had to *leave* my country. He said He would do what He promised when He spoke to me in the classroom in Costa Rica and told me to learn Spanish - give me a work among Spanish-speaking people. I never had another doubt before we drove our heavy-laden van out of our driveway and headed for Costa Rica. Everything was "go".

The next miracle was the sale of our house. We needed the money in order to get to the language school, register and buy books, and provide for one year of living expenses while studying full time.

In 1976, the sale of houses in Denver was at the worst point it had ever been. Real estate felt the sudden "bust" experienced by the energy market. The boom in the oil business in Colorado suddenly vanished like smoke in a heavy wind. The developers had overbuilt new homes, and the influx of homebuyers that the authorities promised would migrate to Denver, never materialized.

Despite the gloomy market I was confident God would help us sell our house. We had a friend in real estate, and asked her to help us sell it, but reserved the right to try to sell it ourselves. Our beautiful, expensive house was in a very desirable area, well kept and sat on a spacious lot. The best sales feature we had going for us, our friend advised us, was the low mortgage rate, provided a prospective buyer could assume it.

I went to the president of our bank, whom we knew quite well, and told him why and when we wanted to sell our house. He was very business-like as he informed me my low interest rate was because I was an officer of a company that had a large payroll and did a lot of business with his bank. Also, I was a board member where decisions are made regarding what bank we would use. "There's no way we'll let anyone assume that mortgage. Your buyer, if you ever find one, will have to get new financing, and that could take months. You'll never make it to Costa Rica by August 28. Are you sure you want to take your family down there?" he asked. I don't think he had a personal relationship with Christ, and of course, he didn't know what I knew about God's ways.

As I was returning home, I picked up a "For Sale" sign at a "dime store", put a stick of wood on it, and jammed it into the ground. As I did, I said to God, "You know I need to sell this place in order to be obedient to your call. Now it's up to you. We need another miracle!"

The miracle knocked on our door in about a week. The father of a pastor in our church wanted to retire in Denver. He brought his wife back later that day and she said she wanted our house if we would leave the new refrigerator. I asked them how they would finance the purchase, and he said he would give us a certified check to pay for it like cash. In a week, the deal was closed. I walked back into the bank president's office, asked him to take out the bank's share to cancel my mortgage, and put the rest in my checking account. I was happy to testify how faithful my God is as I said to him, "Guess who's going to be in Costa Rica by the 28th of August?"

At the same time I was looking for a replacement for our Lincoln Mark IV and our new sports car. One was too big, pretentious and gas guzzling for a missionary, and the other was too small for the trip to Central America with our family. We were praying that God would lead us to the right vehicle. I had no clue as to what manufacturer, type, or model year would be best for our missionary career.

After searching used car lots all over Denver, I seemed to always return to a certain dealer who had a beautiful Volkswagen van. I felt the price was $300 too high, and besides, after driving a long-nosed Lincoln with a hood that spread out in front of me like an aircraft carrier, driving a VW van that had no hood at all made me feel like I was sitting in an unfinished helicopter, so I resisted buying it.

I finally told the salesman that I was looking for a car to drive to Central America as a missionary, and he turned out to be a brother in Christ, and said he would lower the price. These two things convinced me God wanted me to have that particular vehicle. God had closed the doors on buying other cars, but had opened the door to buying the van.

The salesman then told me the story behind the scant 13,000 miles that were registered on the odometer of the 1976 van. A retired, widowed friend of his bought it without seats to go fishing in Florida. He built some neat storage boxes on both sides in the back, but he didn't like the way the van swayed when the wind hit it broadside. When he returned, he exchanged it for a passenger car.

We made benches out of the storage boxes by putting soft pads on the lids. These storage boxes made excellent places for storing the small appliances, radios, TV, tape recorder, and other electrical conveniences we carried to Costa Rica. With our two dogs and two children sitting on them, they were not perceived as containers.

Since we had never driven through foreign borders, I sought all the advice I could, and someone wisely said, "Never volunteer any information. Never say any more than you have to when answering questions." No one seemed to think the storage boxes were anything other than benches, and had no idea what was inside. This saved us a lot of duty and hours of hassles at each of the 5 border crossings.

The van ran perfectly during our 13-day, 5,500-mile trip. In addition, we were just one of thousands of similar vehicles in that part of the world, so parts and service were readily available. When we asked God to guide us to the most appropriate vehicle, we had no idea that He would use us to start a literature ministry in El Salvador and this van would make an excellent delivery wagon.

Rose Ann started a sidewalk Sunday school with that van. We'd drive up to a sidewalk and kids would soon gather. We would slide open the big side door to reveal a felt board and other visuals, and the kids would sit on the sidewalk while Rose Ann taught them Bible stories and choruses. I consider that purchase of the perfect vehicle another miracle because God obviously arranged it.

Now that our large six-bedroom house was sold, we had one weekend to get rid of all the furniture. It seemed unlikely that we could sell it in such a short time. The van was packed and we were being commissioned Sunday night at our church. We would leave Denver early Monday morning, August 15. In 13 days, we would be in Costa Rica — right on schedule.

Earlier in the week, I was trying to word a newspaper ad to sell our furniture when the telephone jolted me from my thoughts. "My name is Booth Brown", the caller said in a powerful voice.

"I am a member of the Full Gospel Chapter in northern Colorado, and I hear you're going to the mission field, is that true?"

"Yes," I replied, "We're scheduled to leave next Monday."

"What are you going to do with your furniture?" he asked.

"I thought I'd advertise it for sale this weekend," I replied.

"Well," Booth declared, "I'm an auctioneer, and I'll sell that furniture for you at auction over the weekend, and give you every dime that comes in. I won't charge you anything, and I'll pay for the radio ads. When we're done, by Sunday night, I'll give you a check for everything. You'll be too busy to handle people answering an ad and they won't pay you as much for your things." He was right. Now, is that a miracle, or is that a miracle?

Every piece was gone by Sunday night, and we even had beds for the night because the buyers said they would come after them Monday morning after we left. To this day, whenever we visit friends in Denver, they'll say, "How's it feel to sleep in your old bed again?" Or "That lawnmower I bought at your auction still runs good." Another said, "This china and silverware ought to be familiar to you. I bought it when you left Denver."

We had our retirement fund in the bank along with the equity from the sale of the house, the cash from the furniture auction, and our savings account. No mission board wanted us as missionaries for various understandable reasons, so we couldn't raise support in churches. But we had enough money to be self-supporting for five years if we had no disasters or expensive sicknesses. As good stewards of the money God provided, we wanted to invest it so that we could live off the interest and not use up the principle. This could provide sufficient income for a lifetime career if we budgeted carefully.

We were running out of time, so I arranged a breakfast meeting with a multi-millionaire, who was on our church board. He also served with me on the Christian school board where our children attended. Since he was so successful in the financial world, and had a reputation as a Christian, I felt he would be a good source of advice for investing our money. The meeting resulted in my giving him all our savings in exchange for a personal note so that he could invest the money for big returns, and pay us 11% interest every month, which was 3% more than banks paid on savings accounts in those days. What a relief that was, and it worked out so easily, and in a short time. I had no idea what I had gotten into.

For the trip and for establishing ourselves in Costa Rica, I had taken a lot of cash, a checkbook and some traveler's checks. Each month when my bank statement arrived from the U.S., I eagerly looked for regular interest deposits, but none appeared. The "going out" of our account kept getting higher because of checks we were cashing; but the "coming in" showed no activity, and the balance in our checking account kept getting smaller.

After several months, I wrote our investor to inquire where he was sending our monthly interest checks, but got no reply. I sent a telegram with the same results. I telephoned and was told he was in Europe. These evasion tactics went on for nine months.

Upon finishing language school, we moved to El Salvador, still with no income from our investment. We were getting dangerously close to zero in the bank, our only resource for meeting the basic daily needs of a family of four and two dogs.

I didn't know how lonely it could be living in a foreign land with residence visa permits for missionary work and with support from outside the country, but no income allowed from a job held inside that country. It was very frustrating. I thought I had our living costs assured, but in reality had to eat beans and rice every day and wonder how much longer we could continue to buy even those - plus pay rent and utilities. With no medical insurance, no credit, no borrowing ability, and no mission board to help, I learned how to trust God for health, food, and life itself. Meanwhile, our ministry prospered and was producing a lot of fruit.

Finally, in economic desperation, I used a credit card to buy a ticket to Denver to confront the man. This was after a year of no returns from his use of our life's savings. I sat in the waiting room of his deluxe office on the top floor of the high-rise building he owned, located at a valuable corner of the Valley Highway in southeast Denver. The receptionist said he was not in, and he was sidetracked on his schedule that morning, despite the appointment his secretary gave me for that hour. I could return the next day at the same time, she advised.

The same thing occurred the second day, and the third. By now, I knew I was getting shuffled and deceived, just as with my letter, phone calls and telegrams from Costa Rica. I began to fear the worst - I would never see that money again, and our missionary career would end abruptly. What's more, we had nothing to return to in the United States. I had no choice but to trust God.

On the fifth day, at 8:00 a.m., I was informed that my tricky investor had suddenly flown off to England on an emergency, and wouldn't be back for a week or so. I announced that I would stay in the waiting room night and day until he returned. I came prepared to spend just that day, not seven days and nights, or more. Thankfully, I had a lot of reading material and other diversions to occupy my time, and set about making myself at home in the waiting room. This made the secretaries, accountants, and receptionists very nervous.

With an urge to use the nearby bathroom, I headed into the hall and wonder of wonders, I caught a glimpse of the back of a ghost, or twin brother, of the man for whom I was waiting, slipping in from a back door to the office suite. He was not in Europe and he didn't know I knew it. Did the Lord arrange for me to see this?

When I left the bathroom, I caught everyone by surprise when I hurriedly walked through the double doors separating the waiting room from the office and headed straight for where I thought he should be. No one had time to warn him. When I bursted through the door of his office and he saw me, the ashen color of his face as the blood drained from his cheeks, his wide eyes and open mouth, were worth the trip from El Salvador.

He promised to have all the money in my bank account the following day, which coincided with my scheduled return flight to El Salvador. I shouldn't have counted on it, but I left hoping it would happen. I was still concerned about how I would get the money reinvested for the highest possible interest, so that we could continue our ministry and not use any of the principle.

The money was never deposited. It was at this time that the new Full Gospel Business Men's Fellowship Chapter we started in El Salvador was having its kick-off dinner in the deluxe, five-star Camino Real Hotel. Our Salvadoran friend, Max Mejia Vides, was its first president. When the Latin American Director, Albert D'Arpa, arrived from Miami to christen the chapter and give us our charter, he stayed with us in our home.

After the big inauguration brother D'Arpa was having his last meal in our home, and he started asking a lot of questions. "You live very humbly here," he observed. "Don't you get much financial support?"

I explained the problem about our life's savings, and how I felt it would be wrong to sue a brother in Christ. Wisely, he said, "My Bible says that you know a brother by his fruit. The fruit he exhibits is not of Christ it is satanic. God wants you to live here and continue the literature and other ministries He has called you to. Satan does not. This fellow is the instrument satan is using to shoot you down and drive you out of El Salvador. If I were you, I'd find a good lawyer in Denver and sue the man immediately."

Upon that advice, I found such a Christian lawyer who got our money from the defaulter without going to court, and who also agreed to reinvest it himself at the same return of 11%, to be paid monthly. Thus, we were able to stay on in El Salvador, and eventually improve our standard of living.

3
WHY EL SALVADOR?

We were ready to start our long journey to Costa Rica. The van was greatly over loaded with things tied on top and on the rear. Every nook and cranny was stuffed with something, and only a little space was left for our six-year-old Christopher, nine-year-old Teri Ann, and two dogs.

Christopher was always hyperactive, and it was difficult to keep him happy enclosed in a small space. He was the kind of little fellow who climbed a light pole while waiting for the light to change. Needless to say, we had to stop every so often just to let him run and climb a few trees, and let the dogs run while we ate a picnic lunch.

Our lovable Doberman Pinscher named Jezebel was nervous the entire thirteen days on the road. She thought stray cows were big dogs trying to usurp her territory. Every time she saw one through a car window she became hysterical and uncontrollable. She ran over anyone in the car to get in a good position to deliver severe warnings of vicious growls and annoying barks at the "trespasser". We finally devised a system where we would warn the children when we were coming to a stray cow. The child closest to Jezebel would cover her eyes until the threat was over. There are hundreds of strays on the highways in Mexico and every country south of Mexico, so Jezebel traveled a lot with her eyes covered.

Latin Americans, in my opinion, have no sense of danger. They don't see danger in many of the things that North Americans do. We saw many pickup trucks fully loaded with people, with most of them sitting on the edge of the truck bed, or on the tailgate. "Don't follow so close", my wife kept cautioning me, "one of them might fall off that pickup." "Be careful of that toddler playing on the edge of the highway" was another frequent admonition.

I can remember when I was in grade school. The teachers were always harping about which side of the road to walk on, how to cross a street safely, or how to safely ride a bicycle. They even had police officers talk to us, some of them brought trained dogs to emphasize the lessons. They don't do that in Latin America, and the more we drove, the more obvious it became.

We arrived in Vera Cruz, Mexico in the evening tired and dirty. We pulled into the motel we had reserved at random from a bland list of names. Our spirits lifted when we saw the waves roll onto the beach as moonbeams danced on their crests. Bathers frolicked and our children squealed with delight. When we got up the next morning and saw the Gulf of Mexico almost at our doorstep, we decided we all needed a well-earned break. We had been driving pretty steady for six hot days and Chris and Teri couldn't have heard better news. I couldn't tell if it made them, or our two dogs happier. Even our hard-driven VW van seemed to feel the respite would be good for it too.

It was a beautiful, sunny morning at 8:00 a.m. in August of 1976 when we sat down to breakfast. The rising sun painted a golden glow on everything in the city square. The city was alive with people going to work, waiting at bus stops or just getting organized for the day. I had never been in a Spanish-speaking resort area before. This was a new and exciting experience. I was enjoying the exhilaration and wonderment of the moment while seated with my family at a sidewalk café. This café was an extension of the restaurant at a beautiful old hotel on the busy downtown city plaza. Until that delightful breakfast, Vera Cruz was just one of the many overnight stops on the map we would have to make on our journey. Latin American countries were nothing special in my mind; I just knew there was a place in one of them where we would eventually settle down to a new life of service to the people on behalf of Christ. It was still in the Lord's hands, and He hadn't revealed to us where that special spot was.

We had left Denver about five days before. What made that particular morning so memorable, however, was the realization that I was finally experiencing the flavor of Latin American life. The pure pleasure of being able just to eat breakfast so late in the morning added something to the magic of the moment. It seemed that all my hyper life, I was well into a day's work by the "late" hour of 8:00 a.m., or hastily driving someplace to make a sales call, if not on a plane flying off to a destination that held the promise of more business.

Added to the fare that made the memory so vivid was the marimba music that filled the whole square with its percussive, rapid, Latin rhythm. There was even a strolling violin player heading our way as he lingered at different tables, hoping that someone would subtly signal him to stay longer and play a requested number - all this at breakfast!

Financially, I shouldn't have signaled to the violinist, but romantically I wasn't thinking of the cost. I had him play "La Paloma" for Rose Ann, while our children sank low in their chairs embarrassed and giggling at the attention we were drawing.

We were eating breakfast in the open air, in a sidewalk café on the town square, right in the middle of one of Mexico's famous tourist areas. It was no longer a popular attraction to North Americans because Acapulco, Mazatlan, Puerto Vallarta, Yucatan and Guadalajara had been built up to entice the Gringos. But the Mexicans still love good, old Vera Cruz as a vacation playground, and I could see why.

We amused ourselves by watching the people as we ate tortillas, beans, rice and scrambled eggs. In the park across the plaza were two young lovers. There were others just as obvious, waiting at a bus stop clinging to each other like vines. A young couple was walking slowly through the park, arms around each other as if to keep each other from falling. Some were at tables there in the café eating and romancing. How could I keep from reaching over to the chair next to me to hold my own sweetheart's hand? Broad, white-toothed smiles lit up the many dark faces, and laughter punctuated the music like tambourines jangling while an orchestra plays.

Little kids were everywhere: selling newspapers, shining shoes, wiping windshields, or begging.

But this is not a travelogue on that grand old city. Vera Cruz, as it turned out, was just a memorable stopover where I began my love affair with Spanish people and their time-forgetting, romantic culture.

"I'm going to like this part of the world." I thought for the first time, as I took in all the action, happiness and romance. Up until then, I hadn't thought at all about whether I'd want to live in a foreign country. Liking it or not never was a consideration because we had a "call". We simply had to respond to the mandate the Lord had given us, and we didn't consider any options. Now I suddenly tasted of Spanish culture, and thank God, it was good! Happiness, romance and lots of action are the formula of life in countries south of the U.S. border.

It seemed the rest of the trip went a little easier after that stop. We tried strange fruits from roadside stands, and admired the sugar cane that looked like fields of ostrich feathers because the cane was in bloom.

Traffic, on the other hand, was not quite so tranquil. Buses and vans zigged and zagged around with the doors wide open. In the cities, we saw blind or crippled people standing in the middle of a busy street, waiting for the light to turn red so they could approach the stopped cars. They didn't consider it dangerous. I don't know how the passengers on the buses could stay so calm when the driver would take them down the left or middle lane, and then suddenly crossover to the right lane to pick up or discharge someone without giving a signal. Street vendors, some only 5 or 6 years old, walked around the flowing traffic, intent on selling instead of watching. This was more evidence that the people didn't fear danger, and we always had to watch out for others while driving.

Despite these traffic differences, thirteen days after we left Denver we arrived in San José, Costa Rica. Some missionary friends welcomed us and led us to our new address. We were to live there, as their neighbors, for about a year while I studied Spanish.

I soon discerned that the people of Central America are not afraid of work. Those from El Salvador, especially, have a reputation for being hard workers. Poverty is rampant. The people work hard to try to improve their circumstance. Unfortunately, many of them believe they have to steal or take unfair advantage of others to get ahead. This often leads to lying or conning. North Americans are quite vulnerable to such tactics. In Costa Rica and wherever we lived, we had the feeling that our house was being staked out for possible illegal entry.

We rented an apartment in Costa Rica, and I took Spanish classes every morning for four hours in the missionary language school. Meanwhile, our two children started school in a private, bi-lingual Christian grade school, until we could no longer afford the tuition. We had to switch them to a school where all the lessons were in Spanish. They adapted quite well. In a few months, they were rattling off Spanish, while I couldn't even ask where a bathroom was.

Because God told me to learn Spanish, I had it in my mind that it would be easy. If He told me to do it and I obeyed, I reasoned that He would make it easy. Was I ever wrong!

I learned that when you're obedient to God's commands, it doesn't necessarily mean He will give you special treatment, special faculties, or favored resources to carry out His will. I remembered how Moses obeyed the Voice from the burning bush, and had years of struggle to accomplish what was commanded. Abraham had a similar experience. The Apostle Paul was obedient to God's will, and got stoned, whipped and suffered other offensive trials. In other words, God obviously considers obedience a normal Christian way that doesn't deserve special recognition. He expects it from His children, and come what may, they get their blessing from the anointing and peace that comes with being in His will. My own experience is that God will give you whatever you lack to carry out His will - but not necessarily anything extra.

Learning Spanish was very humiliating, but I needed lessons in humility. All my adult life I made my living with a glib tongue, whereas in class for four hours every morning, and very often for the rest of the day while dealing with Costa Ricans, I couldn't speak a sentence of that gibbering language. I was mute. It was painful, frustrating and discouraging. Another missionary and I were much older than the other students and while struggling to compete with the fresh, young brains, we hung onto God's promise, "I can do all things through Christ who strengthens me."

Was I sure God wanted me to learn Spanish? I wondered. I was known as an impetuous person. Had I jumped at this conclusion impulsively? Was my brain too stale and un-teachable? Why was I really doing this? What would happen to my family if I couldn't grasp this subject? The devil often tormented me like he did Eve in the garden: "Hath God said?"

In the meantime, I applied to every mission agency in the published Missions Directory, and still no one wanted us. The negative replies usually referred to my lack of Bible School or Seminary training, being too old, not of their denomination, or never being ordained nor having served as a pastor. Where would we go, and what would we do after almost a year of Spanish lessons?

A mission board appointed the five other students in my particular class. Those young, recent college graduates were learning Spanish fast while I looked dumber and dumber and felt like a hopeless moron. I was subjected to an avalanche of senseless words and phrases day in and day out. Homework was difficult and took a lot of discipline. I was too tired at night to study, and with the Costa Rican pleasant weather beckoning me to go outdoors, I struggled to get my assignments done in the afternoons.

Of all the 200 students in the institute, my wife and I were the only ones who didn't know where we would serve and live the following year, nor what we would do. There were constant parties and outings to which we could not be invited: such as a meeting held for all the Baptist missionaries, a prayer meeting for all the Assemblies of God missionaries, a weekend retreat for all the Wycliffe missionaries, a tour for all those going to Venezuela or some other country. We didn't fit in anywhere. What a lonesome, forgotten feeling we had. But we hung in there because of God's grace, and because He said we should.

Then one evening we got the call from missionaries in El Salvador to come there and start a literature ministry. "We don't need any more pastors or evangelists here," they said, "we need a business man who can set up a distribution system of Christian books and Bibles, train the people to run it, buy the materials, sell them, change the money into dollars, and buy more." It was a direct answer to our prayers, and we prepared for the move to El Salvador immediately, despite the much-publicized outbreak of a civil war there.

My wife knew El Salvador well, and often talked about it. Like any macho husband, I'd pretend I knew all about it rather than admit to her that I never heard of it before. I found a National Geographic map and dusted it off, gingerly unfolded its crumbly sections, and there in our garage where Rose Ann couldn't see me, I found the little country, surrounded by the much larger nations of Guatemala, Honduras and Nicaragua. It didn't look like much to me.

When I located it later in an atlas, I discovered that it was the smallest and most densely populated nation on the American continent with about 6 million people. It was very rural, the people spoke only Spanish, and about 14 wealthy families controlled the country. These families usually made sure a military man was its president before the war. The description further told me it was 90% Catholic and 70% of its population lived in poverty. It seemed like a terrible place to live; as if this was going to be my penance for some malfeasance I had committed sometime in my past.

When we boldly left Denver a year earlier, we had no idea that we would end up in El Salvador, much less would be starting a ministry importing and distributing literature. We had absolutely no pre-conceived notion of what we would do, where we'd live or any plans of starting a missionary agency. We went to Central America purely on faith. Naively and innocently expecting God to show us each step of the way. And He has! *One step at a time.*

Three short years later, in 1980, we were still living in San Salvador when El Salvador was at the height of its war. We needed a name for our agency. That's when we said to our faithful friend, Arch Decker, whom we fondly refer to as our "Archangel", "Let's call it Harvesting in Spanish." We wanted to use the acronym "HIS" for the new mission agency he was helping us establish. Even then we naively only saw the establishment of HIS as a convenience for giving receipts to potential donors. God had other plans. It was not our design in 1976 to become missionaries so we could establish our own agency and mission board. It just never occurred to us. God just carefully led us *one step at a time*, by way of necessities.

Here's what I mean by "necessities." As we served independently in El Salvador, we tried to help the thousands of needy children who were suffering from wartime tragedies. As we sent word back to the States about the ways we could help the homeless or abandoned children, donations were mailed to us. We needed to give receipts, but we had no system. Arch Decker said any receipt we would give at that time allowed no tax deduction for the donor. We had to have tax exemption approval from the Internal Revenue Service. To do this, we needed a non-profit corporation. Once that was formed in 1980, with our archangel serving as chairman of the board, we finally were granted a tax exempt 501c(3) status by the IRS in 1981, and Arch Decker has been the Board Chairman ever since.

To produce tax-deductible receipts and to keep records and books, we needed an office. In 1982 we returned to Denver to set up the office and care for Rose Ann's aged parents. We also wanted to provide a U.S. High School diploma for Chris and Teri. We were unable to get volunteers to run the office, so we stayed on in Denver for awhile, getting more and more entangled in the daily routine of running our mission. Thus, we needed to send missionaries to El Salvador in our place to continue the work we started. And so it grew to what HIS has become today, a sending agency that operates a large children's home, churches, a school, four bookstores, a Christian literature distributorship, and outreaches to street kids, and those living on the city dump.

We acknowledge that God expanded HIS by way of many partners who responded to our many needs over the years. We thank them for being so faithful. As He has with our rapid progress, God seems to be doing a quick work everywhere in these last days.

God blessed this ministry.

Starting from nothing, HIS is now the largest literature ministry of its kind in El Salvador, spreading the Gospel through books, bibles, Sunday school literature and textbooks. These materials are used for the Bible Schools operated by many denominations.

The Bibles, books, and tracts we distribute are anointed to win many souls to Christ. They help pastors preach better, assist them in establishing new churches, and equip Sunday school teachers to teach better. The mission of all these materials is to bring more people to know the Father, Son, and Holy Spirit. Our devotional books have inspired many families to start an altar in their homes.

We're looking forward with anticipation to the next 10 years, perhaps the last decade in the history of earthly human beings. Maranatha! He's coming soon.

4
SAVED FOR WITNESSING

One day our neighbor, Debbie Drake, who was a movie actress and business owner, announced that she had to go to Hollywood to tape TV appearances on the popular Johnny Carson talk show. Because she would be away over the weekend, she asked me to take the children to Sunday school, and I readily volunteered since I would be home that weekend.

That memorable Sunday morning, November 21, 1971, I sat patiently in my car in the jammed parking lot of Calvary Temple, Denver, Colorado, waiting for the children to be released from their class. Then from the sanctuary, I heard the beautiful choir music waft on the air, and my thoughts returned to the orphanage, where I sang in the choir at the Sunday morning services. I was drawn mysteriously to the church service.

Curious about what was happening inside, and reasoning that I might as well spend the hour in there rather than sit alone in the cold car, I made my way to a seat way in the back of the huge sanctuary, where I heard Pastor Charles Blair talking about a small bird called a "Paraclete." I thought he said "parakeet", and nothing he preached made sense. But, as the service drew to a close, I felt hot tears running down my cheeks. I was so embarrassed, and I feared that someone would see me shedding tears of weakness, hardly the best image of an executive. The Holy Spirit, Whom I later learned was called a "Paraclete" in Greek, was wooing me to accept His precious Jesus as my Savior. I quickly repented of my life style, and a tremendous lightheartedness came over me as my burdens lifted. I felt free. I gladly promised God that I would live for Him from that moment on. And I have.

I remember driving home from church that memorable day, with my little daughter Teri and her playmate staring at me almost with fear. I was so overjoyed with my new-found salvation, and felt comforted by the sincere promise I made to God that my entire future was His to do with as He wished. I was shouting, singing and praising the Lord at the top of my voice. No wonder the children were so frightened!

"What's wrong with you Daddy?" Teri cried as loud as she could to get through to me. I came down from heaven, applied the brakes and pulled over to the side of the road. I explained that while she was in a Sunday school class, I had turned my life over to Christ. Though I don't think they fully understood why that called for such joy, the two then infectiously laughed and rejoiced with me, as we turned toward our home in the Cherry Hills area of Denver. I didn't know it, but my fancy car and big house would come to mean very little to me as I grew in the Lord.

At that time I was the Vice President of Marketing and board member of a fast-growing, successful manufacturer that marketed its industrial products internationally. Ambition and a burning desire for wealth and recognition drove me. No doubt it was because I was born in poverty. I never would have dreamed that in five years I would be leaving friends and family and the comfortable profit-making world for a nonprofit agency in a poor nation, to carry the gospel to strangers in another language. I was the "up-front", very visible image of the company, with an open-ended expense account that I used and misused, throwing lavish parties for our sales personnel and our representatives from around the world. I traveled in high style, and helped setup factories in Japan and Mexico.

Our management was convinced that for a growing business to capture an increasing market share in its industry, it was necessary to provide liquor and lavish gifts to the right people. Each board meeting was held with a liquor bar to encourage good communication and camaraderie. Of course, our products and policies were superior, our deliveries reflected good service, our administration was superb and our sales force was stupendous — and my life style was stupid. Now I know that our nasty practices were not as necessary for successful marketing.

I stopped smoking, cursing and drinking the following Monday morning. The word around the office was that I was going through a mid-life crisis and had suddenly got an itch called religion. When I scratched it, they said, it would go away. They didn't understand that I had begun a wonderful relationship, instead of getting religion.

My love affair with Jesus grew rapidly. I bought all the audio cassette sermon tapes I could find, read all the Christian books I heard about, and was in church every time the doors opened. I went to other services and prayer meetings in between. Every time I went on a business trip, I tried to tie it in with a trip to a Christian seminar, or attendance at a well-known church in the city of my destination. All this time I was asking God to show me how to get out of the business world and into a Christ-centered ministry. I didn't want to be a "spectator," I wanted to "be in the game," so to speak. I began to yearn to get on the front line in God's army.

I had been in Atlanta the week before my salvation experience. At that time our Alabama representative, Georgia representative, and our own company's southeast area sales manager, joined together for a meeting with me in an expensive restaurant. We traditionally followed up such a meeting with dinner and entertainment for which I usually picked up the check. After a delightful gourmet dinner washed down with some alcoholic beverages, we went out on the town. As I look back on such escapades, I know now that God was mercifully watching over me. I never had a drunken accident, a fight in any of the bars, or an attack from anyone. I believe it was because God watched over me until I became His servant instead of the devil's.

It was after I returned to Denver from that trip that I "accidentally" attended church for the first time in many a year, and I experienced my conversion on that glorious day that I already told you about. (The Bible says that little children shall lead them and my daughter and her playmate caused me to be in church that great day). The following weekend I was due to go to Miami, Florida to attend a convention, and I noticed that on the return I had a stopover in Atlanta. Immediately the Holy Spirit began to prod me to take advantage of the opportunity, and do what I knew would be the right thing. Because of my short career as a born-again Christian, most people still knew me as the same old rabble-rouser, and I had to come out for Jesus in a public way. I had to witness to the same fellows I had caroused with a week before in Atlanta, and tell them what Christ had since done for me.

Before leaving for Florida, I called our area sales manager in Atlanta and told him I would be stopping off in his city on a certain date to make an important announcement. I asked him to call together all the people who were at the previous meeting and set up a dinner reservation for all of us. Probably thinking I was going to announce a better commission rate or a new product, they gladly accepted my invitation.

I had been praying for the necessary courage to be a strong witness, and for the proper words to say, but I still didn't feel it was going to be easy. But my prayers were answered.

"Dick," I said to our area sales manager, after we settled in our chairs at the swanky restaurant that he had selected, "did you know this is the same restaurant where we last broke bread together?" He hadn't realized that. "Fellows," I said, "Do you realize that we are all sitting at the same table and in the same seating arrangement?" After glancing around, we all chuckled. "But," I began, "We're not all the same people that sat here a short time ago." There was dead silence. I asked the Lord under my breath to cause someone to make it easier to say what I longed to say, but only silence and an unusual look on everyone's face was the response. Some people would not have found such an experience so difficult, but these were important business people to me, and I felt uncharacteristically humbled, and didn't know how they'd respond, or how it would affect my job performance.

I finally blurted out, "Since I saw you guys last, I got saved, and now I'm a Christian."

"Praise the Lord!" said the one from Alabama.

"Thank God," said the Georgia representative, and the ice was broken. All of us accepted Christ since our last meeting except our company's area manager, who was a good Catholic. The fellowship flowed instead of the booze. The Alabama fellow told how he had been teaching the men's Sunday school class for years in the Methodist church he attended, and the previous Sunday, the same Sunday I got saved, he went home from church dissatisfied. He told his wife that there had to be something more to Christianity than he had, and he was going up to the bedroom and intended to stay until the dryness left him. He asked her to fix dinner for the rest of the family and forget about him until he came back a changed man.

"I prayed and wept, and cried out to God to fill my hungry soul", he told us. "After 2 or 3 hours", he said, "I began to rejoice and praise God as a warm peace flooded over my whole being. The next thing I knew, I was trying to tell God how wonderful He is, and how much I love Him, but I couldn't say it in English. I was jabbering away in some strange language, and I almost made a hole in the bedroom door as I rushed downstairs to tell my wife. She was standing at the sink, having finished washing the dishes, and as I came up to her, I couldn't believe my ears! She was standing there looking out the window over the sink at the beautiful sky, also speaking words I couldn't understand. We tried to talk to each other, but we couldn't speak English so we hugged and cried in our unfounded joy.

"The next day I called the manager of your distributorship in Georgia and asked him if I could meet with him in Atlanta before we came here for this dinner tonight," he continued. "I knew he was a liberal Southern Baptist, and I wanted to witness to him. I flew over, and he met my flight, and also made a commitment to Christ. It was wonderful," the Alabaman gleefully testified.

Needless to say, we didn't go partying afterward. All of us went back to my hotel room for a joyful experience, instead of cheap fun, where we fellowshipped about the Lord. The Alabaman told me before he left for home that night, that someone directed him to a chapter of an organization called Full Gospel Business Men's Fellowship International (FGBMFI), where someone explained what happened to him and his wife when they were speaking in a new language.

"Don," he told me, "You have got to have that experience. I'm going to mail you some books. They'll be numbered on their covers in the order I want you to read them. In the meantime, find out where the Denver chapter of FGBMFI meets and attend their fellowship." I slept like a baby that night, in euphoria even while asleep, as I realized what God had done to make my first witnessing experience so blessed. (That Alabama man, now retired, is still one of our biggest, most faithful supporters.)

5

FOREIGN MISSIONARY WORK BEGINS

We were living in an apartment located in the middle class "Los Colegios" section of Moravia, an upscale, newer suburb of San Jose in Costa Rica. We were attending the Instituto Espanol de Idiomas where I was learning the fundamentals of the Spanish language, and Rose Ann was taking some advanced lessons to expand her fluency in it. I was over 50 years old at the time, and beginning a whole new way of life, a new career, in a strange culture in a foreign land with a foreign language. It was an exhilarating new chapter in my life, and at first, the daily challenges made me feel like a kid leaving home to go to college.

After being in Costa Rica a month, the Holy Spirit began to make us wish we could get involved in some kind of a ministry. In fact, we seemed to suffer from an itch, and the only relief would be to start to do missionary work It seemed impossible because of my inability to communicate with the Spanish-speaking Costa Ricans; "Ticos," as they are fondly called. As the itch grew worse the Lord impressed me with the idea that to get relief, I should start a Costa Rican chapter of the Full Gospel Business Men's Fellowship International (FGBMFI). I had been quite active in that ministry in the United States, and had a special appreciation for the organization. For one thing, I met Rose Ann there, and also fellow members only a month before had helped us get to Costa Rica.

We confessed to Bill and Hilda, some wonderful American neighbors who were seasoned missionaries in Costa Rica, the burden we felt to get involved with the people in the community. They witnessed favorably to it, and Hilda agreed to assist us in getting a neighborhood meeting organized. She knew a lot of the people in the area, spoke Spanish fluently, and felt the need for a Bible study or some type of neighborhood outreach. Hilda arranged with a lady in Los Colegios to use her exercise gym, attached to her house, as our first meeting place.

We hung some hand written notices on telephone poles in the area, talked it up with the neighbors, and prayed God would send people. Of course, they never heard of an FGBMFI meeting before. But since most of them considered themselves Christians, being Catholics, they liked the idea of a Christian businessman coming from the United States to meet with them. Obviously the Holy Spirit had used their curiosity to bring so many together, for I was amazed at the turnout.

We began by introducing ourselves, prayed, and then Hilda led some Spanish choruses. Just as I was about to pray again and give my testimony through an interpreter, a man who arrived late made his way haltingly to the remaining empty chair, interrupting me.

"Let us pray" Hilda interpreted for me. "Pray?" thundered the latecomer. He stood up, and was weaving. I realized he had too much to drink.

"I thought this was a business meeting about marketing", he shouted. "This sounds like a religious meeting, and I don't have anything to do with religion!"

"Why not?" I asked naively.

"Because I'm the biggest sinner in this room," he responded, trying to put one foot in front of the other to make an exit.

"Please sit down and hear what we have to say," Rose Ann told him. He was helped back into the chair by those seated near him, as he was saying: "In fact, I'm the biggest sinner in the whole world; God doesn't want anything to do with me. He knows how bad I am."

"That's the first step to getting your life right with God." Rose Ann told him, "Knowing that you're a sinner and need to be cleansed of your sinful past is the start of repentance."

He sat down and remained quiet as we proceeded with the rest of the service. His name was Mr. Baez. The attractive owner of the gymnasium explained apologetically at the close of our meeting that she had to go to Panama the following week and we'd have to find another place to have the next meeting.

I was shocked and pleased to hear Mr. Baez invite us to his home for the next meeting. He told us all how to find it, so we had a firm commitment about the place of our next get-together. As he left he sheepishly said he enjoyed himself, and wanted to see the meetings continue. Somehow I felt God had His hand on him and Mr. Baez was going to give up sin for sainthood.

The following Thursday evening we gathered at Mr. Baez's big beautiful home. More came than at our first meeting and people sat on the floor elbow-to-elbow. Others filled all the chairs and some were even standing. While we were fellowshipping before the meeting, Mrs. Baez, a beautiful, middle-aged, petite lady, made us welcome, and even placed some plates of delicious Costa Rican cookies in strategic places.

Rose Ann got the meeting started by having everyone pray together. Different people who had come with Hilda prayed for God's Spirit to move in our midst, and then I prayed in English for the people present, asking God to heal anyone in our midst who had a physical problem. My simple prayer was sharply interrupted by the joyful shout in Spanish of a young man seated on the floor, "I'm healed! God just healed me! I don't have any more pain in my knee." He had jumped to his feet, and was flexing his left knee. Hilda asked him to tell us what happened to him.

It seems that he had a football injury several years before and he could hardly walk with that leg because of the constant pain. His doctor told him he needed an operation that he couldn't afford. He had resigned himself to living with the pain, and getting around with the help of a cane and sometimes a crutch. He told us that he couldn't remember why he came that night or how he heard of the meeting. He lived in another town a long bus ride away. No one in the room knew him.

After we praised God together, Mrs. Baez came from a dark corner of the room, where she had been observing everything. She wanted to be sure the young man had been healed. When she was satisfied, she retreated to her corner to watch the rest of the meeting.

As the meeting drew to a close, and Mrs. Baez and her maid began to serve coffee to everyone, her husband made a startling announcement. "You know," he said, "I've stopped drinking since the last meeting. I'm beginning to feel better about myself, and I feel there is hope for me." We told him most of us had been praying for him all week. He said that his home would be too small for the next meeting because he would be inviting more people. He invited us to meet the following Thursday evening for our third service, at his office where he had a large conference room. We gladly accepted.

It was then that Mrs. Baez stepped out into the center of the room while some people were leaving and others were still drinking coffee. "If God healed that young man's knee, do you think God could heal my leg?" She asked innocently.

"Of course," we assured her. "Would you like us to pray for God to heal your leg?" "Yes, please," she pleaded.

Several of us gathered around her and laid hands on her. I again prayed in English because I hardly knew five words in Spanish. I forgot to ask what was wrong with her leg, and since she had on a pantsuit, I couldn't see anything. We just prayed and agreed together for her healing and then went home.

The following Thursday we showed up at Mr. Baez's office for our third meeting, and found that he headed the largest advertising agency in Costa Rica.

People were late this time because they had trouble finding their way to his suburban business.

While we were waiting, several of us began to chat with Mr. Baez and some guests he had invited. By now I was able to understand a little Spanish, with Rose Ann helping me. We learned that Baez's guest was a prominent lawyer named Max who had been expelled from El Salvador. This was in 1976, and the world was beginning to hear rumblings of war breaking out in that tiny country. In fact, a young American Catholic priest came from El Salvador and had joined my Spanish class at the Institute. He talked a lot about what was happening over there. While our small group was waiting for the others to arrive, Max began to expound about Marxism.

One of the members who had been coming to the meetings each week, crossed the room and put his finger almost on the lawyer's nose, and said, "Sir, we're not here to talk about anyone else, except Jesus."

"But Marx has more to offer our people than Jesus," replied the exiled lawyer.

Then Mr. Baez startled us all when he put his hand on his friend's knee, looked him straight in the eye, and said, "Max, if Marx can do for anyone what Jesus did for me and my wife, we'll follow him. Until then, we'll follow Jesus."

"What did Jesus do for you?" asked Max. More people came in to the room as he said, "My life is getting better. You know that my wife, who is a doctor, had a weeping cancer on her leg for two years that wouldn't heal. These people prayed for her and God healed her."

I was flabbergasted at what I heard, and asked Mr. Baez to tell us about it while more people were still arriving. "Well," he said, "We went to bed after all of you left the meeting last week. We didn't see any change in my wife's leg. However, the next morning, as we were getting dressed in the bedroom, I looked at her leg and did a double take. The ugly sore was gone, and there was new skin where it had been. Not even a scar. My wife didn't realize it herself until I told her." Everyone praised God and agreed to follow Jesus instead of Marx.

It was God alone who performed that miracle for Mrs. Baez. I could hardly speak the language and was practically helpless to minister. That's how our missionary work began in Central America. Its been miracle after miracle ever since. The FGBMFI Chapter has grown rapidly, and still wins souls to Christ. Mr. Baez died shortly after, but he died as a believer.

Not long after we arrived in El Salvador, the Lord impressed me again with the desire to start a chapter of the Full Gospel Business Men's Fellowship International. This desire was confirmed when I met a bilingual advertising man in El Salvador, named Max Mejia Vides, who had found Christ. Max came to the Lord when his sister, living in the United States, attended a FGBMFI Chapter meeting. She picked up a Voice Magazine published by the Fellowship, and mailed it to Max in El Salvador with a note advising him to read it. Max followed the instructions in the magazine explaining how to accept Christ as his Savior, and made a commitment to live for Him the rest of his life.

Max was always hungry for more of God and soaked up all he could by reading the Scriptures himself and meditating on them while the Holy Spirit revealed their applications to his life. He grew rapidly in the grace and knowledge of the Lord. He had a desire to live a life consecrated to the Lord, and to see many come into the Kingdom. These two desires led him to cancel all advertising he did for liquor and cigarettes, and stop using seductive poses of women in his films. In addition, he began to invite other businessmen to his home for dinner while he explained the Gospel to them.

The dinners kept getting bigger, so he had to move to restaurants to accommodate everyone. It was at this time that we entered each other's lives, to become good friends for life. I explained what FGBMFI was all about, and he was thrilled. He recognized that it is the same organization that published the Voice magazine that led him into Salvation through belief in Christ.

I explained how we had FGBMFI Chapter meetings in the United States, and soon we started Saturday morning breakfast meetings at the largest hotel ballroom in El Salvador. In the meantime I applied to the headquarters in Costa Mesa, California for a charter as a legitimate chapter.

Hundreds began coming to the breakfasts for which we made a charge to cover the costs. In a country that was considered about 95% Catholic in denomination at the time, the people found a place where they could go that was not forbidden by their priests! A hotel ballroom sounded very generic and acceptable – in fact somewhat inviting and intriguing.

We printed up little invitation cards that those attending could pass around to colleagues, friends, customers and their superiors. More and more came, including hundreds of women and young people. Finally we had to divide the people into three rooms – the men filled the main ballroom, the ladies filled a little smaller ballroom, and the young people filled still another one.

Because there was a charge for breakfast in this 5-Star hotel that was way above the price an ordinary person in El Salvador would even think of paying, only those that could afford the fee were coming. As a result, we were reaching the upper crust of Salvadoran society. Military men, government officials, factory and business owners, coffee barons, doctors, lawyers, dentists and other professionals were being baptized in the hotel swimming pool every Saturday after the meetings. These influential people made waves for Christ in their daily activities, and a revival was in progress. This Fellowship was a major factor in changing the religious demographics from 1% Protestant in the previous 100 years to about 25% Protestant in the last 20 years.

We were soon soliciting charters for new chapters starting up in cities outside of the capital and there is a chapter meeting in every major hotel and restaurant in San Salvador. Max served as the national representative to the headquarters in Costa Mesa. Chapters began to flourish in Guatemala after several Christians from that country visited El Salvador. This Christian Business Men's movement is active in every country in South and Central America, and they still all meet once a week instead of once a month as in the U.S.A. Members pay a fee to join, and pay for their meals and an offering is also requested. Because there are so many chapters, the largest ballrooms are now only filled when the chapters come together 4 times a year. There is also an annual convention held in each country once a year, and an international convention of all Central American Chapters once a year in various countries on a rotation basis. As a missionary endeavor, it is different. Instead of reaching the poor, this ministry reaches the middle and upper class, and it has always been self-supporting. I praise God that He laid these Costa Rican and El Salvadoran Fellowships on my heart, and thank Him for involving Mr. Baez and Max Mejia Vides, and for bountifully blessing this thriving ministry.

6
GETTING STARTED IN EL SALVADOR

After nine lonely, arduous months of studying Spanish at the missionary language school in Costa Rica, a missionary called us from El Salvador. He explained that the war had started there, and there was a possibility the guerrillas could overthrow the military regime and establish a Communist atheistic government. He asked if we would be interested in moving to El Salvador to open a Christian literature distribution ministry. He explained that in countries where Communism was established, Christian literature and Bibles were banned and burned. The borders were closed to replacement shipments, and he wanted a stockpile of Christian literature and bibles in El Salvador in case that happened.

My spiritual antenna went straight up. Here was the call we were praying for. Here was the fulfillment of what missionaries Paul Kaufman and Gene Martin told us when we went to the altar at Calvary Temple about a year ago.

"Why did you track me down?" I asked over the phone.

"Because", the caller said, "We don't need any more preachers, evangelists or Bible School teachers. We need a businessman who would know how to buy literature, import it, warehouse it, distribute it, exchange the money, and pay for it"

This was exactly what I had been trained to do. Isn't God good? And I didn't need to be part of a missionary agency to do what was needed in El Salvador, or be ordained, or be a Bible school graduate.

In El Salvador in 1977 only about 1% of its 5 million population, (50,000 people) were born again Christians. The missionaries were very concerned about the lack of sufficient reserves of study books for the Bible Schools. Material was needed to train pastors, and other literature for the growing Christian population. Bibles were also needed. Fifteen years later there were almost 6 million citizens and 25% of them were born again Christians, about 1.5 million believers.

At last everything began to fall into place. Since we weren't under any agency authority, we could leave language school and go to any country we chose. Our lease was up on our apartment, the children's school classes had ended for the 1977 vacation, and the FGBMFI chapter we had started was now being carried on by Costa Ricans. The missionaries had a small, low-rent home reserved for us in El Salvador if we arrived by the end of August. We knew it was God's perfect timing by the way everything fit together.

By now, after nine months of frustrating, intensive language study, I was ready for a change. I would just about go anywhere we were needed where Spanish was spoken. Even though news was leaking out of El

Salvador that a war had started, as a family we were anxious to get there, and start the much needed literature ministry. It sounded tailor-made for us.

We sold everything we couldn't transport to El Salvador in our van, and hit the road. We drove north over the same route we had used to get to Costa Rica many months earlier. On that trip, we were on the last hot days of an exhausting 13-day journey from Denver, so we didn't observe much of the interesting parts of Nicaragua and Honduras. Now, in retracing our route, we saw many things that caught our attention and made the miles go faster. It helped that I could now understand most of the Spanish road signs too.

Driving through the northern ranch country over dusty plains in Costa Rica, through dirty Nicaragua and sweltering, agricultural areas of Honduras, was only made bearable by the intriguing thought that we were heading toward the assignment God had prepared for us, or prepared us for...I wasn't sure which, perhaps it was both.

We observed a lot of the women walking very upright with their cargo carefully balanced on their heads. It seemed to help their posture immensely. The females learn to do this at an early age because it leaves their hands free to hang onto little children, and carry other items under their arms as well as overhead. You never see a man doing that: men carry things on their backs or shoulders. It's a cultural difference.

Women are generally considered by many Latin macho men to be less wise, weaker, and less worthy than men. Many men, we learned, bully the women, ignore their suggestions, and insist on being attended to regally by them. Men in the lower economic level often don't get married. Many move from bed to bed and produce babies by different women.

Fathers' Day is hardly noticed. The children often don't know who their father is. However Mothers' Day is recognized for six days because it's the mother who raises the child alone or with her mother. Very often the grandmother receives a lot of attention on Mothers' Day. We've learned that the mothers usually work as a maid, in an office, picking coffee, and so forth, or go to the United States to make more money, and leave the raising of her children to grandma.

Middle and upper income men commonly have mistresses, though they are very discreet because it is not well accepted by their families. Instead of leaving their children with grandmothers, these men are able to provide nannies, and those children know the nanny real well as they grow up. The nanny is often timid about disciplining the boss's youngsters.

Women are just beginning to assume a larger role in the economy of Latin America. The universities have a high percentage of female students, and are producing female doctors and lawyers. Women in other professions are becoming increasingly more common, and they're generally good at their work.

At the border crossing from Honduras to El Salvador, there were many sour-faced soldiers standing around with fingers on the triggers of machine guns. We saw many soldiers along the highways, and armed guards at every gas station and store. It was an oppressive sight. However, we arrived in San Salvador on schedule and unscathed. The little house that would be our new home, was being held for us after the former missionary renters moved out. The landlady was happy to be able to rent it without a vacancy period.

When we drove into San Salvador, capital of El Salvador (which translated into English, means "Holy Savior" and "The Savior"), we were taken to our new home by the waiting missionaries. The house was very humble, but quite acceptable to a van full of tired travelers. As we followed her in, our well-traveled Doberman checked it all out and gave her approval. Low cost homes in satisfactory neighborhoods were extremely hard to rent, and since we didn't have much money, we were grateful for the arrangement.

After sleeping on the floor of the empty house overnight, we started early the next day by unloading the radio, cameras, TV, typewriter and similar gear. We made a list of essentials we would need in order to settle in. The local church we would attend sent a young lady to help us clean up the house. She watched our things while we went shopping.

Soon after we drove out of sight a young man rang the doorbell and announced to the cleaning lady; "Brother Benner sent me to pick up his radio to have it repaired." The young lady thought, "well he called him brother and knows his name, so he must be legitimate", and so she let him in. At gunpoint he forced the girl to stay in the kitchen while he carried out everything he could lift. Someone at the church, a painter, a worker or someone just lingering, heard us check in, overheard the directions given to our house, and took advantage of a great opportunity to enhance his economic status.

Welcome to El Salvador! This was only the first of many robberies we would experience in the years to come.

We learned that it was acceptable to rip off "gringos". We learned to always let a Salvadoran ask on our behalf the price of something, or get a quotation by fax or mail so the supplier couldn't see our blue eyes or hear our strange Spanish. This is not said in bitterness. We adjusted to the system, and followed the cultural guidelines as we learned them.

It was time to furnish the house. We needed a good old-fashioned American garage sale, but instead we had to search classified ads and buy as best we could the items we needed. Much of our needs were being filled at the market on our shopping trips. We were learning a lot about various sections of the city during our search for furniture and furnishings. Rose Ann was always talented in making a place "homey" and this peculiar house was no exception, even though it seemed like the builders deviously designed it to make it as challenging as possible to furnish.

Then we began to "itch" to start our literature ministry. We felt the Holy Spirit impressing on us that the need for literature was urgent.

When we greeted Mr. Carlos Valiente, a wealthy Christian, we knew we would enjoy working with each other. He was an avid soul-winner who had a burden to see his wealthy friends saved. His Catholic friends would not go to the church he attended, so he bought a large space in a beautiful, new shopping center and put up a sign that read: "Auditorio Josué", which in English means "Joshua Auditorium". He held services on Sunday afternoons. Having a lot of empty space in the big room, he willingly gave us a corner of it, rent free, to start our literature ministry. The Lord provided a rent-free place while we were low on funds: He provides in various ways. Money wasn't always necessary to do God's work.

We made a little profit on the furniture and other things we sold when we left Costa Rica, and hadn't paid any tithe on it yet. When we offered it to the pastor of the church we began to attend, he said that he believed that the Lord wanted us to use it to start our ministry. We bought our first books and Bibles with it.

Carlos Valiente's church began to grow rapidly as many accepted Christ every week. The larger the attendance, the more Bibles and books we sold. Soon there wasn't room for both of us. He needed more space for folding chairs, and we needed more space to hold our growing inventory. We mutually agreed to go our separate ways.

Auditorio Josué was renamed Iglesia Josué, (Joshua Church) when it was accepted into the Assemblies of God denomination. It is now one of the largest churches in El Salvador. They meet in a beautiful church the congregation built in a wealthy neighborhood without missionary funds from the U.S.

Our little bookstore moved into a very desirable space in the main shopping center where there was a lot of shopping traffic. Here is how we got there.

We are accustomed to moving ahead on faith when we know what God wants us to do. The decision to go from a place with no rent, to an air-conditioned store in the high rent district of the largest and most modern shopping center in Central America, took a lot of faith. We barely had enough money to live on and still had no missionary support. We adopted a strict policy that we would take no income from sales in the bookstore. We could not afford to pay anyone in those days so we tended the bookstore ourselves for long hours. Though we now employ about 30 Salvadorans in our literature ministry, we still do not take any income from it.

When we left the auditorium location, we prayed much about where to relocate. The impression we kept getting is that God was showing us a particular store that the tenant had vacated. The owner was refurbishing it for new renters.

We contacted the owner, and learned that the rent would be at least $800 a month, (15 years later we were paying $1,500 a month). The $800 was a huge sum considering our financial resources. It loomed even larger when we realized our steady customers were now moving miles away to attend the new Joshua Church. But we felt confident that we were obeying God and that He would provide what we needed to occupy a retail store. We also felt that God would give us success in this location, and that He would enable us to get a lot of Bibles and Christian literature into the hands of Salvadorans. No Christian book store in Latin America had ever been located in a shopping center before.

When we inquired about the possibility of renting his space, the owner said it would be a couple of months before the location was ready for occupancy, and that he would add us to the growing list of those who were applying for it. Our confidence really began to wane when we learned that such prominent corporations as Levi (pants), and Arrow (shirts), among others, were vying for it. It was the only vacancy in the popular new mall.

We continued to pray and in faith set money aside for the initial maintenance deposit and the first month's rent. We passed by the store many times per week, observing the progress of the workers inside and claiming it for God's work. One day there were no workers around and it appeared finished. No one called us and no one moved in. After three weeks of anxiously wondering who would be awarded the "privilege" of renting it, we were finally able to phone the owner at home. He was a Jewish man who lived in another city. When we inquired of him as to whom he was going to rent it, he expressed surprise that we still had not taken possession of his store.

"I thought my secretary called you a month ago, before I left on vacation," he said, "but I guess she forgot. You can move in, and I'll come by and get the paperwork handled. Get the key from the shopping center office."

Elated, we immediately moved from the church to the new location and prepared to serve the shopping public. At first it was a struggle to make the monthly rent payments, but in 23 years (as of this writing) we never missed one, nor were we late.

It was a much bigger store than the little corner in the church we formerly occupied. We filled it up by building bookshelves and buying more books. We purchased a sign and cash register, among other things, to complete the store. People were not lined up at the door to buy our Bibles and books. We were totally dependent on the Lord to provide —and He did. At first we had to sell most of our household furniture and some of our appliances to make the rent payments on time. We found that sitting on wooden crates and eating at a card table was no big deal. The food tasted just as good, and our children found it as humorous as we did.

Gradually, the bookstore prospered. It became a focal point for the Evangelical community in El Salvador, and a congregating place for the North American missionaries serving in that country; and many years later, it still is.

Soon after we opened, a banker who had an office on the top floor of the landmark high-rise office building in the shopping center, had his chauffeur park his sleek Mercedes Benz at our front door. The banker, who looked like someone from an Esquire ad, emerged from the black car and surprised us by coming into our young bookstore.

"I saw your sign go up when I was looking down on you from my office," he said. "As a banker, I'm always interested in the types of businesses that open around here. What do you do here?"

We explained that we were a ministry, not a business, and that we sell Bibles and Christian books. "You mean that you can support your operation just on sales of Bibles and books?"

"Do you have a Bible?" I asked.

"Yes, but it's a Catholic Bible."

"That doesn't make any difference. It's the same as the ones we have here, except that yours has a few more books in it that don't really change the message in the others. Those additional books don't really add or subtract from anything that is in these Bibles," I assured him as I gestured to our shelves full of all kinds of Bibles.

"Do you read your Bible?" I asked.

"I tried to once, but I can't understand it very well," he replied.

"When you get to know the author of it personally," I explained, "you will not only understand it, you will read it with enthusiasm."

I pulled Tim LaHaye's book, *How to Study the Bible*, from the shelf and handed it to him. "Take this book as our gift, and read it with your Catholic Bible. I'm sure it will interest you."

A week later he returned. "I really got a lot out of the book you gave me. Do you have any others like that?"

I explained God's plan of salvation, and told him that the Bible was God's love letter to him. He would understand it when he accepted Christ as his Savior."

"That sounds good but I'd like to read another one of your books first".

We had just received the Spanish version of Charles Colson's first book, "*Born Again*". We found that affluent people in El Salvador followed the Watergate fiasco, and liked to read Colson's book, so I gave him one. A week later he returned, his face aglow, (all smiles), wanting to commit his life to Jesus. He subsequently was made president of the largest bank in Honduras, and he moved to that country. Several times a year, on his visits to El Salvador, he would pop into our bookstore to say "Hello". As far as we know, he is still a deacon in a very active evangelical church in Tegucigalpa, Honduras.

This is just one example of how the Lord uses our four bookstores in ministry. I visited a church in San Salvador where I had not worshipped for a long time. After the service a man approached me, and said, "You're Donald Benner, aren't you? You used to work in the Joshua Bookstore, didn't you?" Then he proceeded to tell me how he was looking in the window of our bookstore one day years before, and I went outside to talk to him and gave him a Bible.

"I threw the Bible on a shelf at home and never opened it until three years ago when I got into a desperate situation. I remembered what you told me, came here to the church and gave my heart to the Lord. I am a leader here, my wife is active with the women, and my five children are all in Sunday School. I've been wanting to thank you for a long time."

One day a young man came to the store full of joy. "I was in jail and one of your workers gave me a Carothers book, *Prison to Praise*. I became a Christian and now that I'm on the outside, I want to give that book to a lot of men I know who are still in prison." He walked out with ten copies and regularly came back for more, full of conversion testimonies of prisoners to whom he witnessed and gave a book.

Just recently an usher said to me as I entered a church, "I've been wanting to tell you thanks for a book you gave me 18 years ago. It started me on my successful search for salvation."

I remember listening to a sermon on a cassette tape right after I gave my heart to the Lord and the preacher made the statement that God was always there when he got discouraged. Then God would plop a great, big, juicy grape in his mouth (referring to a pleasant spiritual experience) that would encourage him anew. I never forgot that anomaly, and learned that God would do the same for me – praise His Name! These occasional references to things people experienced through our ministry are like juicy grapes plopped into a hungry mouth.

One of those times was when we were feeling a little "dry", like our missionary work seemed to be stagnant and not exciting. As our church service ended one Sunday a man approached me, his hand outstretched with a warm greeting.

"Aren't you Donald Benner?" he asked me.

"Yes," I responded, "Who are you?"

He gave his name and said he was a dentist who had accepted Christ through reading a book I gave him once when he came into our bookstore. Francisco moved to San Francisco to practice his profession and he and his wife began a fruitful ministry among the Spanish-speaking population there. While visiting his family in El Salvador, they came to our Shalom Children's Home and they and their daughter ministered in a powerful, memorable way to the children.

Trinity Broadcasting built a beautiful new studio in El Salvador under the guidance of my friend Max Mejia Vides. I introduced Max to Paul Crouch, the President of Trinity, when Paul first came to our country. When it was finished Max invited me to come see it and to give me a personal tour of the facilities. As I walked out of the reception area into the hallway with Max, a young man grabbed my hand and started hugging me. "Max," he said. "This guy is my spiritual father. I accepted Christ when he gave a testimony at a meeting I attended several years ago." He was the sound engineer on Max's staff.

These are just two examples of how God "plopped a grape in my mouth" to encourage me when I needed it. A friend from Merrit Island, Florida, named Robin Little, often visited us. He was a great encourager. One time I was eating breakfast with him at the hotel where he stayed, and was moaning to him about how hard it was to raise the funds necessary to properly care for the children in our children's home. I had just read an article in the morning paper about a truckload of supplies that was donated to a well-financed Catholic orphanage, and assured Robin that we needed such a donation more than they did. Finally, I really showed how sorry I was feeling for myself by telling him how hard it was for an inter-denominational, small, inconsequential mission like ours to get recognition and acceptance by churches.

Robin interrupted my pity party to tell me that just that morning he was praying for us, and God gave him a Scripture for us. It was from Zechariah 4:10 "Who despises the day of small beginnings?" It refers to the Temple of the Lord, which started small, with a good foundation before the visible walls and roof were added. Small beginnings are normal and necessary Robin said, and when God is in it, the small beginnings are the foundation for the more prominent things to follow in due time. His sincere words were a great comfort and encouragement to me.

Another time we felt the Lord wanted us to return to the United States to report to some of our supporters what the Lord was doing in our ministry. Sometimes I am not sure whether a trip like that was my idea or God's. I was ready to get away from El Salvador for a while, and I wanted to enjoy the orderly way things are done in the States. Also, I wanted to get back to my own culture like a fish returning to water. I wanted to hear my first language all around me, and escape the insanity of the political war we lived in daily. That's why I had to be sure it was God's idea.

At that time, our Salvadoran workers were well trained, and they urged us to make the trip. Taking that as a sign that God was leading us to make the long, dangerous, 1,500-mile drive to Denver. We had to go through areas of Guatemala where there were a lot of battles and where many people were ambushed on the roads. Then, Chiapas State in southern Mexico followed, where a lot of guerrilla activity was reported. We had to have God's approval and protection, especially since we were taking Teri Ann and Chris with us. They had no choice but to go when and where we did.

I discussed with Rose Ann several times where we would stay once we arrived in Denver. We had sold our home and no one we knew had space to take in the four of us and our Doberman. It would deplete our budget if we had to stay in a motel for the four months we expected to be there. The answer was always the same: trust God, He will provide.

Our tired family arrived at the little 4-room house where Rose Ann's mother and father lived. We rejoiced about the long, uneventful trip just completed. We slept on the floor and couch for one night, then Ralph LaBarr, an old friend, called and said he had a large two-bedroom furnished apartment just vacated. He offered it to us rent-free and even paid the utility bills. You see how faithful God is to provide our needs when we are walking in His will? It was a beautiful, quiet place, well decorated and complete with dishwasher, washer, dryer and every other appliance we could wish for. Our God is good to His Children.

It was the Christmas season of 1980 and Rose Ann told me that she was going to buy a good camera for my Christmas present. I had lamented that we had no decent photographs that captured our work to show our supporters.

We visited a lot of friends and relatives, and spoke in a few churches. During the Christmas rush we began to shop for a camera, and soon learned that the kind I wanted was too expensive. I told the Lord I wanted a Canon 35mm single lens reflex camera with a telephoto lens, and a flash attachment. I had been taught by the well known, Dr. David Yonggi Cho, the Korean Pastor, to be specific when I prayed for something. Late Christmas Eve we were lying in bed, and Rose Ann said, "I'm sorry Honey that I couldn't afford to get you the camera as your Christmas present."

Don't worry," I responded, "It just means that its not God's timing."

We began to drift off to sleep when the telephone jolted us back to full wakefulness. "Is this Don Benner?" a soft voice asked.

"Yes. What can I do for you?"

"You don't know me, but my name is Gordon White. I was in the audience when you spoke at our church last week. You apologized for the poor quality of your photographs and your camera. At that moment God spoke to me and said, "Give him your camera!" I couldn't believe what I heard because photography is my only hobby and it's important to me. I had just bought the camera, too. Well, I fought the idea for a week now, and I've been losing sleep. My wife said to call you now, even though it's late, and Christmas Eve. But I'm anxious to be obedient and get peace in my soul." He apologized for not being obedient sooner.

"Oh, Brother White," I said, "I'm so happy you called. My wife wanted to get me a good camera for Christmas, but we just couldn't afford it."

Mr. White told me to come to his house the next day, which just happened to be Christmas day. "Come for dinner," he said, and gave me directions to his house.

"Tell me Gordon," I asked him, "is it a Canon?"

"Yes."

"Is it 35mm, and does it have a telephoto lens?"

"Yes, how did you know?" he wondered.

"I'll tell you tomorrow afternoon when I see you. We have a commitment for Christmas dinner at noon, but we'll be there in the afternoon about 3:30."

When we arrived at Gordon's house, we were all rejoicing together: Gordon, because he had such a peace about giving up his prized camera; and us, because we had been the recipients once again of God's love and grace. "Gordon is a new Christian," his wife confided to us. "He found it hard to give up his new camera, and he had to be sure that God really wanted him to do such an unusual thing – give his cherished camera to some strangers."

A short time later we packed up for our return trip to El Salvador. I was making some last minute calls, to say good-bye and express our thanks for all that our friends and family had done to make our visit enjoyable, restful and successful. One of those calls was to Gordon White.

"I'm glad you called," said Mrs. White. "I want to tell you what happened to Gordon the other day. The husband of a member of our church died, and Gordon and I went to visit and pray with his widow as well as offer any help we could. As we started to leave, she asked Gordon if he knew anything about photography. When he told her about his hobby, she invited us to the garage, where she had put her husband's camera equipment. It was also his hobby. The lady told Gordon to take all the camera stuff because she didn't know how to use it and wasn't interested in learning. Gordon hasn't come back down to earth yet. The camera was much better than the one he gave you, and it included other equipment he always wanted to own. He is so glad he obeyed the Lord even though it hurt when he gave you his camera."

Before we left Denver to start the long trip back to El Salvador, I felt that I ought to buy an extra car battery and an extra fan belt. Our vehicle now was an old Ford Van with a good engine that pulled a whole lot of metal parts that rattled and shook a lot. These two items, I realized later, were purchased under God's guidance. As we were driving along a lonely road across a hot desert in Mexico, the engine suddenly heated up.

When I stopped, I found that the fan belt had broken. If I hadn't had the spare, I would have been in real trouble in the hot sun on a sparsely traveled road where bandits often roamed.

Later in the trip I stopped at a busy gas station to get some fuel. After paying the bill, I turned the ignition key and nothing happened. I was under a lot of pressure from grumbling customers lined up behind me to get away from the gas pump. The little station only had two pumps and I was occupying one of them.

The station attendants pushed our van out of the way and went back to pumping gas. The van's lights wouldn't turn on, and the horn wouldn't blow. The engine's alternator had not been generating electricity for the battery, and so the battery was dead. The gas station had no auto parts and no mechanic, but told me there was a Ford dealer in the city about 15 miles ahead. That spare battery was a blessing. I replaced the dead one with the new one, and was able to start the engine and make it to the Ford dealer, where the mechanic discovered it was only the low-cost relay that had burned out and not the more expensive alternator.

As we crossed the busy border from Mexico into Guatemala, I began to wonder (just like when we were on our way to Denver at the beginning of this journey) where were we going to stay when we arrived back in El Salvador? A hotel in the capital is very expensive, so we began to pray about it. We asked God to provide a place, and show us how to get it.

Decent hotels in foreign territory are hard to find, and at four o'clock in the afternoon we passed a nice looking motel. Not knowing when we would find another acceptable place to stay overnight, we thought it would be prudent to stay at that one even though it was rather early for us to stop for the day. We turned around to get a room for the night, figuring we'd start early in the morning to drive on. Our children and Doberman slept in the van and we rented a room for ourselves. We parked by our room, unloaded our bags, and headed for the dining room.

After we thanked God for the room and food and asked Him to bless our meal, some people called to us in English. It was some missionary friends from El Salvador who were retiring and going home to California. We asked if they knew of a place for rent in El Salvador, and lo and behold the house they had left that morning in San Salvador was available; and at a rent we could afford. They called the landlady from the motel and she agreed to hold it for our arrival the next afternoon. See how God takes care of His children? A bonus was the productive garden the missionaries had created behind the house.

Thirteen years of our missionary service in El Salvador was carried out during war that affected almost every family in the country. Many families suffered from a loved one being killed, kidnapped, or wounded by serving in either the government or guerrilla army. As the fighting got more ferocious and dangerous, the U.S. Embassy pulled all the families of its personnel out of the country, and eventually left only a skeleton crew in El Salvador. They published a bulletin advising all North American citizens to leave because they could no longer be responsible for their safety. At that time the missionaries working for denominations and mission boards were ordered by their headquarters to leave as soon as they could. Our family was able to stay because we were the members of our own board. There were a few other independent missionaries who also stayed, as well as an independent Baptist family, a few missionaries with the Central American Mission, and a Nazarene family.

The U.S. Embassy had established a system of communication so they could disseminate information rapidly and get it to every American possible. Each area of the Capital, for example, had a "captain" who had a list of the telephone numbers of all the Americans in his area. The embassy phoned messages to the captains and they forwarded them to the people on their list. Messages like, "stay in your home today, there is a reported uprising expected", or "stay out of the Soyapango area" were common.

We used that grapevine to organize a missionary breakfast meeting at a hotel to see who was still around, get acquainted, and discuss how long we felt we should stay in the country. It was fun fellowship and a great time of prayer. Lively discussion developed about whether any of us would leave or stay the course. We all acknowledged that every missionary ordered to leave by his mission board, did so reluctantly, and only out of respect for the authority over them—not because they wanted to leave. Pentecostal, Baptist, Nazarene, or whatever, meant nothing to any of us. For the duration of the war, we fellowshipped warmly as brothers in Christ.

One missionary told how Salvadorans respected him because he didn't leave when he had a good excuse to. Another said his message was being received with more anointing because Salvadorans told him he had preached we should always trust in God, and he was practicing what he preached by staying in the country. Still another testified that many pastors asked him to stay because this was the time when they really needed his teaching, encouragement and counsel.

I told the group how God had given me Acts 18:9-10 some time ago when I was praying for guidance about leaving or staying. I read it to them: "Do not be afraid; keep on speaking, do not be silent. For I am with you, and no one is going to attack and harm you, because I have many people in this city."

Every one present accepted that verse as God's Word for them also, and adopted the promise as their own. Other fellowship breakfasts followed among the unlikely companions. Pentecostals, Baptists, and Nazarenes joyfully prayed, ate and fellowshipped together. The war brought all the believers together. We're still good friends though some are scattered around the world on other assignments through their missions.

One time I flew to Los Angeles to meet a Christian Brother for breakfast at the Denny's restaurant in the heart of Hollywood. As we wound up our visit, he asked me what he could take to the Lord in prayer for us. I had spent quite a bit of time explaining how just my wife and I were doing most of the work of the mission, and we needed some help. This was a burden on my heart – would we be able to get the people we need to support the steady growth in our mission?

My friend and I prayed about it in the restaurant, and he promised to continue praying about it. After leaving him, I snaked my way around the freeways in the rented car, and headed to a large independent church in Ventura several hours away. As I drove thoughts kept going over in my mind. I began analyzing and praying for the people we would need for our growth.

When I arrived I was led to the mission pastor's office, hoping to present our work to him and get the church's support. During my presentation, the pastor started talking. "Don," he said, "I must interrupt you. Please excuse me, but the Lord is impressing me with a Scripture for you. It is Isaiah 43:4," and he opened his Bible and read this to me:

"Since you are precious and honored in my sight, and because I love you, I will give men in exchange for you, and people in exchange for your life. Do not be afraid, for I am with you; I will bring your children from the east and gather you from the west."

A few weeks later, a lady came to Denver from Los Angeles and made the same prophecy to me, "God is going to give you the people you need, and will bring a lot of children into your life", she prophesied. Then she read the same scripture to me. I was greatly humbled, and my spirit leaped with joy.

The promise of getting men to help in our ministry was always on my mind. We needed to get back to El Salvador to carry on our work. We also needed a staff in the United States to operate an office there.

A year passed by and only a couple of people came to work in our under-staffed Denver office. I still didn't see the promise being fulfilled that I had received by way of the mission pastor in Ventura. However, one Sunday morning in a church in San Salvador, while we were all worshipping the Lord and singing praise to Him, a strong anointing fell on me. It was so powerful I began to weep. As I wept, God said to me, "You have been looking for people in the wrong place. Look for people for your ministry here in El Salvador, not for people in the USA."

A wonderful peace came over me as I received this revelation. Sure enough, as I thought about our growing staff in El Salvador, I could see God's fulfillment of His promise.

One of the promised ones was Angela Cruz*. Gentle and soft-spoken, she was an excellent manager of one of our bookstores. Working with Angela as a cashier was Marta*, a lady who accepted the Lord as her Savior in our home. Marta married a pastor, and was expecting a child.

Shortly before her baby was due, she became sick and was rushed to the hospital. The doctor did everything they could for her but she slipped into a coma. The medical people said they thought they could save the baby, but not Marta.

Rose Ann and I were in the United States when Angela called apprising us of Marta's condition, and asking for prayer. We passed that request on to every 24-hour prayer chain we knew, including the Oral Roberts University Prayer Tower. Churches and friends of our ministry all over the United States and El Salvador were interceding for Marta and her baby.

Early in the morning Angela was awakened by the Holy Spirit, and was impressed with the idea that if she would go to the hospital and lay hands on Marta and pray for her, she would be healed.

---

* Fictitious name to protect the person's privacy.

Angela could hardly wait until the sun came up that morning so she could go to the hospital and pray. Angela was on her way without taking time to eat her breakfast. She entered the room where Marta lay in bed, still, and unaware that she had a visitor.

Angela approached the bed and laid both hands on the form lying there, and began to pray for her healing. An occasional nurse came in and out as she softly prayed. Soon she felt a movement beneath her hands. She opened her eyes and looked into Marta's wide-open eyes. Angela continued to pray until Marta sat up in bed.

The nurses were astounded as they watched a miracle take place. They called the doctor and when he arrived and tried to figure out what happened, he finally agreed that she couldn't have come out of the coma and cheat death except by a miracle of healing.

The hospital kept Marta for several days of observation, and then she walked out on her own. The baby was born a short while later, and he was given the special name "Donald", after me of course. He's probably the only Donald in El Salvador because it's not a Spanish name. The doctors warned Marta not to try to have any more children. She had seven more without any problem – praise the Lord!

In 1991, the peace agreement was signed and the 13-year war ended. Since that time there has been a growing middle class, and more families are living above the poverty line than ever before. There are more schools, hospitals, shopping centers, office buildings and other signs of prosperity.

However, even with all the construction going on, satan has a persistent grip on its people. There is oppression, poverty, disease, illiteracy and misery everywhere. Satan wants to keep it that way, but God wants to change it. And He is changing it with the help of missionaries and pastors. Many short-term missionaries are coming in increasing numbers to help with the spiritual battle. Their greatest hindrance to successful evangelism is the lack of knowledge of the country's culture and language. However, some get so burdened for the souls of the people that they return as career missionaries.

We aliens, who are long-term residents of El Salvador, have the benefit of long-time service and old friends, to help us learn the customs. The difference in the culture of North Americans and Central Americans is often very subtle. I recall a secretary I had who made a cup of instant coffee for me every morning when I got to the office. She seemed to play with it, nurse it, and take too long. Finally I blurted out one day, "Don't waste so much time making a lousy cup of coffee!" Six months later I sheepishly learned that she was making what the office girls called "café de amor" (Cup of Love). It was actually her way of expressing her fondness for me. When I learned this, I was very ashamed of my typical American impatience.

7

WE SERVE A MIRACLE WORKING GOD

I didn't always make good decisions. In fact, I made quite a few bad ones. For example, I was in charge of a stadium campaign where the famous Korean pastor, Dr. David Yonggi Cho, was going to preach. It was at a time during the war when the city was experiencing a lot of killings, kidnappings and robberies. Tension was high. We wondered if people would leave the safety of their homes and if they would be afraid to be among a lot of strangers in a stadium.

What a blessing it was to see many thousands of trusting believers come together to worship the Lord. I incurred a lot of expenses to prepare this event: newspaper and radio advertising, posters, hotel rooms and meals, sound and lighting equipment, and offering baskets. Oh, those offering baskets! I was glad to see all those people and could visualize the baskets running over with money – paper money.

I instructed the ushers to pass the baskets throughout their assigned area and then dump them into a 55-gallon barrel. Two ushers guarded the barrels to prevent theft, and when the offering was over, the barrels were to be taken out a certain door of the stadium where a van would be waiting to whisk them away under the protection of armed guards. They would be taken to our office to be counted and stored until the bank opened the next morning.

The plan seemed good on paper. But paper was exactly the problem. I had not taken into account how many poor people would be there, or how many would come with just bus fare to get back home and a few coins more, so they wouldn't lose much if they were robbed.

The offering baskets were so heavy with coins that they had to be carefully held with two hands so they wouldn't break. The 55 gallon barrels were so heavy that it was impossible for two men to carry them. I had to recruit two more helpers for each barrel so they could be brought down, with a big struggle, to the parked van. The overloaded van sagged under the weight of all those silver coins, and the tires threatened to flatten. Thank the Lord the van didn't have to be driven very far.

At the office the volunteers started counting, and counting and counting. All through the night they counted, and in the morning I had to find other volunteers to take over. And so it went for four days and nights. I was so discouraged when I saw the total of the deposit. The offering only covered about ten percent of our expenses. Oh, yes, the bank! You can imagine how upset their employees were when all those coins were carried in, and they also had to count them to verify the deposit. But at least they had coin-counting machines.

But the campaign was a huge success in terms of what it did for the Kingdom of God. Hundreds were saved, and hundreds were healed of serious illnesses, infirmities and handicaps.

*****

Jorge Raschke, a popular and successful evangelist from Puerto Rico, held another great campaign during the war at the same stadium. Jorge came to El Salvador to meet with the leaders of his denomination, the Assemblies of God. He humbly explained that God had told him to come to El Salvador and hold a campaign in a stadium.

The leaders were skeptical, especially when Jorge told them the only dates he could hold the campaign; the same dates the soccer championships were being played at the stadium, so it obviously would be unavailable.

"Look" Jorge urged the men "apply for the use of the stadium anyway. If God truly sent me here, the stadium should be available somehow." So the members of the Assemblies of God Evangelism Committee wrote out a request and carried it to the government office in charge of the use of the stadium.

The government officials told the Evangelism Committee members that this particular year, because of the dangers of having such big, screaming crowds at night, they had decided to have the soccer matches in the afternoons, therefore the evenings would be open for using the stadium.

The committee was greatly impressed that maybe God had directed Jorge Raschke to come to El Salvador. But the Evangelism Committee's faith was still shaky because its budget was used up and it had no way of financing the campaign. A member of one of the Assemblies of God churches heard about the campaign and the financial obstacle, and said he would finance it. That was not the last miracle needed. The sound system was out of the country, in use in a campaign in

Guatemala. However, a call to the owners revealed that it would be returned in time and it was available on the date of Jorge's campaign. Everything needed for the campaign was coming together.

For three nights the stadium was completely filled up, and God performed fantastic miracles and saved thousands of Salvadorans.

"Why is God filling teeth and healing problems in the mouths of so many people at your meetings?" I asked Jorge.

"I don't know. I've never seen this happen before," Jorge responded.

Apparently this was God's way of authenticating the preaching of His Word by Jorge. I speculated that it was because almost everyone in El Salvador had need of dental work of some kind, so more people could experience a miracle. Compared to those suffering from heart problems, diabetes, arthritis, or handicaps, there were far more who could use a miracle in their mouths.

But who can guess why our Father does miracles one way or another? But he did a lot of oral surgery during Jorge's campaign and accepted thousands of new Christians into His Kingdom.

A mother and daughter from the church we attended went every night. The girl begged her father to go with them, but he just wouldn't. When he heard about all the teeth being filled, some with gold and some with silver, and teeth being straightened, he got curious and agreed to go on the last night.

His beautiful daughter had been in a car accident, and her mouth was in bad shape, and some teeth were lost, some chipped and most were loosened. Jorge Raschke looked up into the section where this family was located and announced that there was someone in that area that needed a healing in the mouth. He invited that person to come down to the front so he could pray over them.

The father went down with his daughter, and while Jorge prayed, the father saw his girl's mouth come back to its normal shape, and there were no chipped or loose teeth in it. She was completely and suddenly healed, and her father gave his heart to Christ right there.

That was on a Saturday night, and the following day in church, when the pastor asked if anyone had a testimony, the father was the first one to get to his feet, and he told what had happened to his daughter and to him. He asked her to stand up. "Some of you know how my daughter looked yesterday. But look how she is today." He then told how he resisted Jesus until his daughter had received the miracle. "So you can see her new teeth, we'll be standing outside the church and anyone who wants to look in her mouth can do so."

After church I saw the pearly white, perfectly formed teeth and beautiful mouth God gave this pretty girl. It was a powerful testimony.

*****

Esther and the other workers at our bookstore on Arce Street, near downtown San Salvador, were dusting, sweeping and arranging books because there were no customers. Soon a man sauntered in and pulled out a pistol. He ordered everyone to gather around the cash register, and put their hands on top of their heads, while he took all the day's income. As he backed down the center aisle toward the front door, Esther said: "You're committing a very bad sin. That money is the Lord's and we are going to pray that you'll bring it back."

After he left, the workers joined hands and prayed for the man's salvation, and that he would return the money. Sure enough, the next morning as soon as the store opened, he came in with the money. He said he had been a Christian, and couldn't sleep and was convicted of how sinful he was. Esther showed him how to recommit his life to Christ.

*****

A Christian druggist in San Miguel asked for some books he could sell in his drugstore. It was too dangerous to drive there during the war so the distributorship sent him a variety of titles via bus. One day, a doctor came in and along with his other items, purchased a copy of David Wilkerson's book *"The Cross and the Switchblade"*. Thrilled with what he read, he returned to ask the druggist to recommend a church where he subsequently gave his heart to the Lord.

A few weeks later the doctor responded to a knock on his door as he was preparing to go to bed, and he was startled to find two guerrilla soldiers with a wounded comrade. Not being sympathetic to the leftist movement, and realizing what would happen to him if the Salvadoran Army soldiers learned that he helped one of their enemies, he didn't want to let them in. When they brandished their guns, however, he had no choice.

The two guerrillas brought the wounded young man into the doctor's living room, and laid him on the floor. Then each took a seat to guard him. One of them ordered the doctor to treat their companion, and the doctor bent over him to examine his gaping bullet hole. He finally bandaged up the wound and began to wonder how he could help his patient spiritually.

The doctor prayed silently for guidance as he looked into the teenager's handsome face, when he was suddenly reminded of the book that had pointed him to the Lord. Noticing that the two guards were dozing, he retrieved it from the top of his desk and carefully opened the patient's shirt. He slipped the book inside and buttoned it back up, and felt he had done what the Lord wanted, so he committed his patient into God's hands.

The doctor shook one guard awake and then the other also woke up. The doctor advised them to put their comrade to bed for several days, and keep him quiet. So one of them lifted their soldier friend over his shoulder and carried him out into the dawn of a new day.

Back at camp, the young man awoke lying on a mat, and felt the book inside his shirt. He pulled it out, and having nothing to do, began to read it. As he devoured chapter after chapter of David Wilkerson's book, a strong feeling of love for Jesus began to well up in his heart.

When he finished the book, he made a commitment to follow the Lord. From then on, he had a desire to get to a church, to return to his family and leave the army he had reluctantly joined.

His family was so overjoyed to have their errant young man back they prepared a fiesta of welcome in their little community. When they asked him to speak, he told everyone about the book. He described how the Lord had become so real in his life, and about the peace and joy he felt in his heart. Eventually, his entire family and many villagers became believers: so many they decided to start a small church. The doctor, who was a new Christian when he gave the book to the wounded boy, also became a strong soul-winner in his own town. This is the kind of fruit our literature ministry bears throughout the country.

*****

Our books and Bibles contributed a lot to sustaining the revival in El Salvador. Our literature helped pastors preach better sermons, and Sunday school teachers reach children more effectively. Our tracts won many souls to Christ, and the tons of Bibles we distributed helped families build a daily altar in their homes. Bible school students studied from the books we supplied and young people read how to be engaged yet sinless. Marriages were healed. Thousands learned how the Holy Spirit works in the lives of struggling Christians, and how timid believers could become bold in sharing the gospel. During the war, when missionaries and pastors could not travel into the extensive war zone, our gospel literature could reach those people on a public bus.

Early in our Joshua Bookstore, we hired an intelligent young lady as manager. She had worked for a long time at the El Salvador Bible Society, and knew most of the pastors and Christian leaders in the country. One afternoon, she recognized a pastor who entered the store looking for a book. Immediately, she left her chair at her desk in the back of the store to greet him. No sooner had she taken one step in his direction, when a bullet came through the ceiling, and went through the seat of her chair. Had she not left it to talk to the pastor, (in fact, had he not arrived to make her want to greet him) the bullet would have killed her. In such ways God also protected my wife and me and those working with us, all during the 13-year war. We will never know how many other times we *were* in danger, and God intervened, until we get to Heaven; but we can testify of many times when we were aware of His protection.

*****

One morning we were due at a Christian school to hold a chapel service with the children. As we carefully drove through the city I suddenly had the idea of stopping to buy cookies for the students.

"Not now," Rose Ann admonished, "We're running late."

"It won't take long," I replied, and stopped the car in front of a bakery.

Had we not had that few minutes of delay, we would have arrived at the height of a fierce firefight between guerrillas and government troops right in front of the school. As we approached the school we found warm dead bodies lying in the street. None of the students at the school were hurt, for they were already in the chapel, lying on the floor and praying.

When our own two children rode the bus to school in the mornings, it was not unusual for them to see dead bodies on the sidewalk, in a yard, or on the street. Their classes often had bomb drills, and the school always closed when bombs went off close by. They had a difficult time in those days because they could only go to school and return home, completely devoid of any outside social life. They were great "troopers", however, and rarely complained. Of course, the confinement did marvels for their grades; their homework was always thoroughly done and on time.

*****

A lady active in the women's ministry once pulled up in front of the church in a brand new car to attend a ladies' evening meeting. Two young men with bandanas over their faces greeted her with guns drawn and demanded that she surrender her car keys. She complied and went inside to tell the ladies what had happened. They started praying immediately that she would not lose her car. They all could hear the thieves trying to start the automobile, but it wouldn't run. Finally they left in disgust. The owner returned to the car, and turned the key that was still in the ignition. The motor jumped to life instantly. God had intervened on her behalf.

*****

A patrol of government soldiers was fighting a band of guerrillas in a village near the Honduran border. Several soldiers on both sides were killed, and finally, the guerrillas retreated into the countryside. The government soldiers climbed into two large army trucks and started down the road away from their encounter.

Soon after leaving the limits of the village, they spied someone running in a field, the low bushes disguising who it was. "There goes one!" someone cried out, and all the soldiers, trained in target practice, began to shoot at the running figure. Thirty soldiers could not hit the person running, and when they realized it, they finally began to laugh at each other and make fun of their lousy marksmanship. They drove on.

Unbeknown to them, the person they were aiming at was a mother who held her baby tight against her breast. When the bullets began to whiz around her, she knelt down and put her baby girl on the ground hovering over her, and prayed for the Lord's protection. While the soldiers continued shooting she stood up and ran as fast as she could to reach trees 50 yards away; but no bullet harmed her nor her baby all the way across the field; not even when she huddled on the ground. She testified later that she kept repeating, "Jesus, save us!" and God answered her simple prayer.

*****

Some Nazarene missionaries, close friends of ours, told us about a nice home near them that had been vacated. It turned out to be exactly what we had been praying for. A three-car garage was located in front of a large room, and both would serve as warehouse space for our literature. The close proximity of a huge water storage tank was our only hesitation in renting the house.

In 1980, Rose Ann and I made a quick trip to the United States and once there, it was tempting to remain and let the trained Salvadorans continue our work for us while the war raged on. One night I spoke at a Full Gospel Business Men's Fellowship meeting and after the service, a friend asked Rose Ann if our house was on a street with a hill, had a certain type fence around it, a large garage on one side, a big garden on the other side, and he continued to describe our newly rented house in accurate detail.

"How do you know so much about our house?" Rose Ann asked.

"Well, God gave me a vision of such a house while Don was preaching, and I figured it was yours. I saw angels all around the house, protecting those who lived in it."

With that reassurance, we returned to El Salvador as the war was escalating. Our son, Christopher, joined a Boy Scout troop, and gradually we outfitted him with the required uniform, hiking gear and manuals. He was excited about the prospect of having new friends and an expansion of his limited social activities.

After about a year, God began dealing with me about moving the inventory from our home to a separate warehouse. We had been enjoying the convenience of having it nearby, where we could work long hours without leaving the property. Here, pastors and other customers, all Salvadorans who were not conspicuous on a street like we Americans were (and thus they were not as vulnerable to kidnappings or shootings), would come to us to get their Bibles and books along with the Sunday school literature.

But God persistently pressured me to move the valuable merchandise, and I not only reminded Him of the convenience and security we enjoyed, but also the lack of funds we had to rent a separate location in addition to and apart from our home.

Unable to sleep at night, and impressed with the urgency to put the stock somewhere else, I finally told Rose Ann about it. She was as puzzled as I was, but said that if I was sure God was speaking to me, we had to obey. On the next Sunday, after church, we were driving around the city of San Salvador seeking a sign from the Lord to indicate where we should relocate the warehouse.

While all this was taking place, a very nice, expensively dressed lady named Annie, had called on us at the house several times to try to talk us into renting her brother's spacious home. He fled to Miami and wanted a North American to live in it. North Americans had a reputation for taking good care of the houses they rent: they even fixed them up, added electrical outlets, and other conveniences, and maintained them well. Salvadoran renters, on the other hand, were known for being a bit destructive.

Finally, to placate Annie, we decided to let her take us to see her brother's expensive house. As we traveled toward it, we drove higher and higher up the hillside, and the air got cleaner and cooler. The view of the entire city and surrounding mountains was spectacular. And so was the house. It was a huge mansion with brass railings, marble floors throughout, a large American-style kitchen with every appliance. It had stereo music piped throughout the house, four huge bedrooms, each with a large bath and walk-in closet, and a dance hall-sized room on the second floor that could serve as a large office. A chauffeur's apartment was attached to the 3-car garage. The drive circled from the front gate to the front door under a covered entrance. The grounds were large, with a spectacular, blooming rose garden, fruit trees, flower lined pathways, and grass that would make a golf course owner jealous. It was very impressive.

After many "oohs" and "aahs," we told Annie that we were modest missionaries, not rich American businessmen. We could not live in such luxury because of what our donors would think. She assured us that the rent would be much less than we were paying for our present house. She just didn't want it to be empty. She wanted Americans to live in it and keep it up. There were very few of us still in the country.

When we returned home, we kept wondering if God would approve of our living in such a beautiful peaceful residence. Was He trying to test us or bless us? We heard enough messages on blessings for God's kids, that we could believe that it might be His will. But we concluded that this was a temptation we should put behind us and dismissed the idea.

However, we still had the haunting feeling that God wanted us to rent a warehouse for the literature. After driving around in a section of the city one Sunday afternoon praying, "Lord, show us where you want the warehouse," we both suddenly felt the same sensation in our spirits when we passed a certain bombed-out three-story building. We backed up and looked it over. The three upper floors were unusable and unsafe, but the garden-level basement floor looked fine. We felt that this was the place.

Monday morning, we drove back to the building and found the owner. He let us look around in the basement floor and in our spirits we definitely knew this was it. He happily rented his "worthless" building to these crazy "gringos" for $800 per month...a sum we just didn't have.

On faith, we signed the rental agreement. God gave me the idea to start another retail Christian bookstore in the part of it that was accessible to the street, and section off the rest as a warehouse and office. With the help of workers from our bookstore in the shopping mall, we cleaned it out, erected walls and painted all the next week. We moved the entire inventory from our house on Saturday and would open for business the following Monday.

That same Saturday, we had planned two other events after moving the books and Bibles to our new location: sending Christopher to his first Boy Scout meeting, and a special dinner at our house for the nine Salvadoran people now working in our ministry. The food was cooking in the kitchen, and we all were outside in various activities. Rose Ann and I were taking a photograph of Chris in his new scout uniform. At that moment, as the camera went "click" a bomb went "BOOM!"

Rose Ann looked at me, wide-eyed, and shouted, "The water tank!" As our house's roof and some walls tumbled down, 250,000 gallons of rushing water flooded downhill from the demolished tank, right through the garage and large storage room, and on through the house and out the other side, carrying small furniture pieces, knick-knacks and debris with it. Everything left inside was soaked.

Had we not moved the $45,000 worth of books and Bibles, they would have been destroyed. The terrorists placed a bomb at the tank to destroy the water system in our area because a member of the ruling junta lived there. But true to the vision our friend had explained to us in the United States, not one of the six of us who lived in the house was hurt beyond a small knick on Teri Ann's chin from flying glass. Angels must have protected us.

As if alerted to the tragedy in advance, television reporters and their cameras appeared suddenly, and we were on the afternoon TV news soon after.

About that time our employees began to arrive for the planned dinner. They looked wonderful in their party dresses and suits. They were unaware that we were in a disastrous situation. Dressed in their best clothes, they immediately began to help us. Some of our neighbors as well as the members of Chris' scout troop also helped out. Strangers helped get the furniture and rugs up out of the water to rest on counters and set outside to dry.

There was no place to sleep, and no security for our belongings. Crowds were gathering and cars were filing by to gawk at the mess. Then Annie showed up with house keys in hand. She saw the news report, and knew she had ready renters for her brother's mansion at last. God got us to accept the beautiful house as our home in a very unique way.

That night we spent the first of many nights in a beautiful mansion, supplied by our loving Father. It was like being on a retreat, away from the war that raged below us. We shared that home with many people in El Salvador that came to preach, teach in the Bible School, or visit with us. We also invited people from the city to come up and spend weekends in our home. Everyone enjoyed it immensely.

Incidentally, since our dinner party was ruined, and our guests were wet and dirty from all the work they did, we made other plans. By nine o'clock that Saturday night, we went to a pizza house to eat and fellowship together. We praised God for His protection and rejoiced over His timing to convince us to move the hundreds of Bibles, cases of tracts, boxes of Christian books, and cartons of Sunday School literature before a bomb sent thousands of gallons of water streaming through their storage area.

Furthermore, God picked a perfect place for our new warehouse and bookstore. We didn't realize that we had moved everything within a few blocks of a large bus terminal that was the base for all the buses arriving from the outer provinces of the country as well as from Guatemala. Also, our new bookstore was located next to a new technical college that opened up shortly after we moved in.

The pastors and customers could now arrive by bus in the capital for their Bibles and books, and get back home by noon. They didn't have to take a taxi or city buses from the terminal to our former location and back, carrying heavy boxes. The new students at the nearby technical college came into our store to photocopy and buy student supplies, which we quickly put on the shelves to help pay the high rent. These students were excellent prospects for the gospel and many accepted Christ.

Isn't God good...and wise? He chose the best spot for our ministry and gave us a lower-cost, more beautiful home to live in.

8
FRAUGHT WITH FRAUDS
Names are ficticious to protect privacy.

Walking through the fields of a farm, we felt the surety from God that it was to be ours. We could see children running and jumping everywhere in our thoughts. We visualized cows leisurely chewing their cud in this field, goats and pigs in pens in the other field, and corn six feet tall swaying in the ocean breeze sweeping in from the nearby beach.

We bought two major pieces of property in El Salvador for carrying out the calling God gave us to work with orphaned and abandoned children. In both cases we made the deals with the owners even though we didn't have any money on hand, the promise of God being our only asset.

In retrospect, we can see that God worked in strange ways to get us the much-needed properties. I would like to be able to say unequivocally that we got the properties on faith because we had no money to buy them, but in a way that is not entirely the case.

In 1982 we began to support a humble orphanage located in the city of Sonsonate, El Salvador. There were thirteen pitiful children that a Salvadoran friend of ours told us about. Miguel was the director of an agency consisting of local pastors who were organized to receive aid for their congregations from sources outside of El Salvador. When he took us to look at the orphanage, which was being directed by a country pastor, we could see that the children needed a lot of help.

In a former lumberyard, we found the children sleeping on the ground in the shed that once stored wooden boards. The stove was a pile of bricks that burned firewood, in an outdoor kitchen. The toilets didn't flush, and ran over onto the dirt that the children used as their postage stamp-sized playground. Their hair was matted, their clothes were torn and dirty, and their hands and faces were even dirtier.

"How could anyone let children live like animals in a pen?" I asked Miguel.

"That's why I brought you here," he said, "will you do something for them?"

"We'll let you know," was our response at that time.

In the following days we were haunted by the sub-standard conditions under which those children from one to ten-years-old, were barely surviving. After praying about what our participation should be, we felt that the Lord wanted us to trust Him to supply us with $1,500 a month to improve the living conditions in that orphanage. This was a huge amount of money to Salvadorans, and to us as well.

Not feeling it wise to give the director that much cash (probably as much as his year's income) we thought it best to give it to Manual, instructing him to buy food, soap, shampoo and such necessities with our donation, and send them to the orphanage.

Right after that, we went back to the United States, where we repeatedly heard from Miguel, asking for more money for the children, stating that we were the only help they had. We started sending $2,000 every month, which was donated by friends and churches. We returned to El Salvador after a long time, and visited the orphanage in Sonsonate. I could see absolutely no difference...no improvement in the condition of the children or the home.

The next day I visited a missionary friend, and explained how frustrated I was with the situation. Bill proceeded to tell me about a missionary he knew in Guatemala called "Bob*" who was helping an orphanage in El Salvador. I got his phone number and called him to see how he was dispensing his donations to the orphanage he was supporting.

"I'm sending the money to a Christian agency that sends supplies to the orphanage for me."

"Is the director named Miguel?"

"Yes, how did you know?"

"Where is the orphanage located?" I asked.

"In Sonsonate," he responded.

"But that's the same orphanage we're supporting," I told him.

"Oh, it can't be the same one," he protested. "Miguel said we're the only one supporting this orphanage."

"That's what he told us, also." I informed him.

I described the orphanage and named the director, and we knew we were talking about the same one.

---
*Fictitious name to protect the person's privacy.

much do you send to Miguel for them?" I asked.

"We send $7,000 a month. How much do you contribute?"

"We send $2,000 a month, and that's $9,000 a month for only 13 children." That's $693 a month per child! A doctor's salary at that time was only $300. "I just came from the orphanage yesterday, Bob, and I can tell you that not one cent seems to be going to those kids. They are filthy, and their conditions are terribly unsanitary. You would be ashamed and embarrassed if you ever took one of your donors there to see that home."

"Don," Bob told me, "I have my own airplane," if you'll meet me at the Ilopango Airport in San Salvador, I'll fly down tomorrow, and we'll go together to confront Miguel with our findings."

When Bob, my wife and I walked into Miguel's office together unannounced, he was flabbergasted. The blood drained from his face, and he couldn't find words to welcome us. We told him how we discovered that he was telling us that each was uniquely supporting the home in Sonsonate. He denied that he was telling anyone else the same thing, and we had no way of knowing if that was true or not.

I also told him about the poor condition of the children I found in my recent visit, and accused him of keeping the money himself. Of course he denied it, and Rose Ann let her Irish temper take over, and she angrily shamed him for what he did in exploiting those poor, defenseless children, and informed him that he wouldn't get another dime from Bob or from us. Following that, we stormed out of his office.

We all felt like a coffee break was in order after such an ordeal, so we looked for a café on the way back to the Ilopango Airport, where Bob's plane was waiting for him.

"This is not the first time we've been defrauded," I told Bob as we settled into chairs in the café.

"It's not my first time, either," Bob admitted.

Then I made a suggestion: "Bob, you're interested in working with a good children's home in El Salvador and so are we. We've both been "burned" by crooked people, too. So what do you say we go together and start our own?" "That's a great idea," Bob suddenly agreed. "However, I don't want to operate it. I'll finance it, but I don't want to have anything to do with running it."

"Perfect!" I exclaimed, "We'd like to operate it. If you'll provide the money, we'll start the home."

"How much money do you think it will take?"

Having already been on the drawing board for such a scenario, I had a ready answer, "It'll take $50,000 to buy a place, establish ourselves legally, equip the building, hire workers and get needy children in residence."

"That sounds great. You look for a place and I'll get you the $50,000!" Bob said.

We shook hands on it, and then drank our coffee while we talked about our experiences of trying to work with children. It looked like we finally were going to have our own children's home — but it didn't work out that way.

While sipping our coffee, I explained to Bob about one of our other unfortunate experiences, which was probably our worst. A missionary friend from the U.S. said to us while he was visiting, "You people are working with needy children and I'd like you to meet a Salvadoran friend who is working with needy children and could use some help." So we made arrangements for him to bring the fellow over to our house in a few days.

The fellow was a nice-looking, very courteous, and soft-spoken young man. I asked him how he met Christ, and he told us this very convincing story in perfect English (but without a British accent, an important observation as you'll soon learn).

"When I graduated from high school five years ago, my family wanted me to be a Catholic priest. They sent me to Rome to study in a Vatican training college. There were classmates of mine from many countries, and every once in a while one of us would ask the professor something about Protestants. We were always put aside quickly and firmly with the advice to stay away from such erroneous sects that were born of the devil."

"When I graduated and was due to return to El Salvador to be ordained as a priest, I decided I would first see a lot more of Europe. I started north from Italy and visited France and Spain, then Belgium and finally across the English Channel to London."

"I didn't know anyone there, so I stayed in a cheap hotel. For the first time in my life I heard gospel music being played on a street corner by some Salvation Army musicians. I couldn't speak much English, so I didn't know why they were doing that, nor did I recognize any of the songs they were playing. They certainly weren't any like those I'd heard in El Salvador or Rome, nor in the occasional bars I visited during my European tour."

"One lonely night I was walking one of London's dark side streets and I heard some people singing and clapping so joyously that I was attracted to it. I followed the happy sound until I came to a plain looking building whose doors were invitingly open."

"My caution lights went on in my conscience, and bells began to ring a warning in my head. Protestants! I thought. People inspired by the devil. But curiosity got the best of me, and I went in to see what these people were doing. The music lifted my spirit, and a man began to preach, but I didn't know what he was saying. However, when people started walking down the aisles toward the front of the building, I felt compelled to follow them."

"Something happened to me when I knelt down in front with the others. Understanding that I couldn't speak or understand English, they found someone who could talk to me in Spanish. I repeated what I was asked to say and later learned that I had prayed to receive Jesus. I no longer wanted to be a somber Catholic priest, I wanted to be a happy Protestant pastor."

"The people immediately took me under their care. I moved in with a nice family, and the church arranged for me to take English lessons and go to a Bible School." (Yet he didn't speak English with a British accent).

Bob interrupted me at that point, "Are you talking about a guy named Cristobal*?" he asked.

"Yes," I replied, "Do you know him?"

---

*Fictitious name to protect the person's privacy.

"Of course, we support him."

"Oh no!" I gasped, "Let me tell you the rest of the story."

Cristobal said he felt led to return to El Salvador and start a Christian School and orphanage. The London church helped him get started. When we met him, he charmed us. We wanted to help him, but said we wanted to see the school and the orphanage first. He repeatedly rebuffed this request by saying that due to the war it was too dangerous to go where the school was in the town of Ilobasco, and even more dangerous to go to Jutiapa where the orphanage was located.

"Have you ever seen his school or orphanage?" I asked Bob.

"No, I was told the same thing," he replied.

Then I told Bob how one of our young Salvadoran employees, named Miguel, wanted to help children, so we sent him to Ilobasco to work with Cristobal and get experience until we got our own children's home in operation. While Miguel was involved in Cristobal's School, he was never allowed to go to Jutiapa to see the orphanage. Miguel also suspected something was amiss about Cristobal. For one reason, Cristobal lived in a deluxe apartment building in the most exclusive residential area of San Salvador, and seldom appeared at the school.

The idea that it was too dangerous to go to Jutiapa was confirmed by many of our friends, but it still sounded suspicious. Even though Jutiapa was in the middle of the war zone where the guerrillas and the soldiers often had furious fire fights, we were determined to get there somehow.

Miguel told us to contact a man he knew that he felt would take us there for a price. At last we found the courageous person who had a 4-wheel-drive jeep and would take us on the scary 2-½ hour trip. We set the date to leave the capital early in the morning so we could leave Jutiapa for the return trip no later than 3:00 in the afternoon. The driver confirmed the rumor that in the war areas, the soldiers were in the field from 9:00 a.m. to 5:00 p.m. After 5:00 p.m. the guerrillas came out to do their dirty work, so it was essential that we be out of the area by 4:00 p.m.

The night before we were to make the dangerous foray to see Cristobal's orphanage, we prayed a lot with different friends and employees. He had said there were 50 children in his orphanage and that's why he asked for a lot of monthly support for the home.

When the driver showed, we loaded up the jeep with 50 stuffed animals, a lot of candy and cookies, and plenty of games for children. We did not know what we would find, but we wanted to let the kids know they weren't forgotten out in the middle of the war zone. We set off without Cristobal having the slightest notion that we were going on the trip.

We wisely left watches and excess money behind. We looked carefully in all directions and thanked God every time we made a blind turn in the dirt road and found no guerrillas waiting for us. The road got very rough, and we were thankful that the vehicle had four-wheel drive.

Finally, we got to the little pueblo of Jutiapa. The driver drove around asking where an orphanage was, but the only directions we repeatedly got were to a day care center. The citizens kept telling us it was the only place where children were cared for.

When we pulled up to the little house to which we were repeatedly directed, an old, thin lady appeared. "Are you Ana*?" I asked, "yes", she replied. We had found Cristobal's "orphanage"!

"We know Cristobal," we told her, "and we brought some things for the children." We were gladly welcomed in, and found 12 nice looking children, not 50 that should have been orphans. Ana revealed that she was operating a day care center for parents who worked, and who paid her so much a day to baby-sit them. Thus we found out why Cristobal tried to keep us away from Jutiapa. We left much of the things we brought for 50 children, and the 12 children were still playing, laughing and joyously thanking us as we made our exit to begin our dangerous return to San Salvador.

While all this was taking place, Miguel was threatened at the school in Ilobasco by some of Cristobal's creditors who suddenly showed up. After promising to get them some answers, he caught the next bus to San Salvador, and surprised Cristobal when he rang his apartment doorbell. The door was left ajar, so Miguel stepped inside while Cristobal went to his bedroom to get some clothes on. It was then that he saw some photos on a desk near the door, and he looked at them. They were photographs of Cristobal in the nude, in pornographic positions with other men.

Miguel met us upon our return to the office from Jutiapa and told how he quickly left Cristobal's apartment without saying anything to him. He said he never

---

*Fictitious name to protect the person's privacy.

wanted to see Cristobal again, and would not return to Ilobasco.

Now we knew the true story about Cristobal and his "orphanage". When I finished telling it to Bob, he was amazed, but grateful. He vowed never again to send money to him. This additional bad experience over children's care made us more determined to start our own place together.

"Find the property, and I'll send the money", Bob said as he crossed the tarmac to his single-engine plane for his return to Guatemala. "We'll be praying for you," he shouted, as he started to climb into the aircraft.

A year before this, one of our bookstore sales clerks told us there was a teacher at one of the Christian schools who was trying to help some children on his small salary. We arranged to meet Marvin*, and he took us to see the children in a small house he was renting in a low-rent district. His fiancée was watching over the 16 children, all seven years old or under, while he was teaching during the day. There was no refrigerator, very little food and no play area. Most of the children slept on the floor since they had no beds.

We knew we had to provide young Marvin with the things he desperately needed to take better care of those children. We bought beds and a refrigerator and filled it with milk and food. Next we rented a larger house in a better neighborhood and stocked it with bags of rice and beans, and arranged to have bread delivered daily. Marvin was very grateful and much encouraged, and he and his fiancée took good care of the children.

Meanwhile, we felt we would be depriving the children in the humble orphanage in Sonsonate if we

*Fictitious name to protect the person's privacy.

abandoned them. We didn't want to punish them just because Miguel was not honorable, and had not given them the supplies due them. We began delivering food, shampoo and other supplies to the children ourselves, and making sure the director put them to use.

By this time we had incorporated in the U.S. as Harvesting In Spanish, and fifteen people were now sponsoring children in the Sonsonate orphanage at $15 a month. At that time the $225 we received was our entire income for the new mission and we were using only $75 of it to translate sponsors' letters, travel to both orphanages, buy stamps and a typewriter, and print sponsorship literature and many other things. Percentage wise it was a lot, but of course it wasn't enough to cover all our start-up costs, and just as is true today, we took no income from the sponsors' donations for ourselves, but obviously used much of our personal funds to operate the mission agency.

One donor in those early days caused us grief because she accused us of keeping 33% of the donations. She didn't know how much we contributed and didn't care. Today our expenses stay around 11% of our total income, and my wife and I personally were the largest donors to Harvesting In Spanish for many years, including church donors, corporations and individuals. Our personal income comes from social security checks and a small investment.

Every time we would get Marvin and the children moved into another even larger rented home, more children would show up, and the home would appear to shrink too small for us to house them all. Sometimes the landlord would make them move because there were too many. In 1983 we moved the orphanage four times, and we also began calling it a children's home instead of an orphanage because we discovered some of the newer children were abandoned instead of orphaned.

A missionary, named Mike*, of the Nazarene denomination arrived in El Salvador from Nicaragua, and we eventually became neighbors in the area where the water tank near our house was blown apart. "If you ever run across a Nicaraguan named Castillo*, who fled to El Salvador with the building fund treasury of a big Nazarene church in Managua, be careful." We filed that information in the deep recesses of our memory bank.

One day a man came into our bookstore where we were working, and told us about an orphanage many miles away, in a town on the Pacific Ocean called Metalío. As soon as we could do so, we made the long, hot trip to Metalío over terrible roads, and finally found the orphanage. It looked pretty clean, and was based in a large beach house. As we waited to meet the director, we observed there were 12 well-cared -for children running all over the place.

A short, middle-aged man appeared, and with a soft-spoken voice introduced himself saying, "Hola, yo soy Don Castillo", (Hello, I'm Mr. Castillo). He showed us around, and we began to like him. We shot a roll of film of the place, and returned home. On the return trip we kept rolling the director's name around between us because it sounded familiar.

I told my wife, "Do you remember what Mike told us about a man from Nicaragua? I believe he said his name was Castillo, the same as this fellow's name

---

*Fictitious name to protect the person's privacy.

whom we met today. Mike said he was in children's work. I wonder if this is the man he told us about."

We had the film developed and showed the photos to Mike, "That's the guy!" he exclaimed, "He not only stole money from a church, he took some movie films of a very nice Christian children's home in Nicaragua and showed it around the U.S. as his own. He, no doubt, opened the orphanage in Metalío with some of the money he fraudulently raised on that trip."

We decided we could not get involved with such a man, and began praying for the children in his care. In the meantime, we were trying to up-grade the living conditions of the children in the orphanage in Sonsonate. The pastor and his wife sold a lot of the toys we brought to the children and kept the money. His three children, all older than the oldest of the children in the home, were very bossy with the orphans, and got the biggest portions of food, and used the soap and shampoo for themselves. While that pastor was the director, the orphans were dirty and unkempt and the situation appeared to be hopeless.

In the meantime, (in 1984), we moved Marvin and the other children three times from January to November. That month Marvin and the children had to leave the home they occupied when the landowner had the water and electricity turned off, because we didn't move the children out as soon as he wanted us to. Neither Marvin nor we knew where to rent a suitable house again. The only place Marvin knew of was a coffee farm way out in the country in a pueblo called Huizucar. So the children were packed up again and were transported to a farm with ripe coffee beans waiting for harvest.

I had been looking for a piece of property to buy ever since Bob from Guatemala agreed to put up the money to start our own orphanage. María, a divorcé whom we were instrumental in leading to the Lord, owned one that interested us the most. We went to visit her property several times, and finally concluded that we couldn't buy such a large piece of land with the $50,000 that Bob said he would supply; and she wouldn't lower her price. We began praying and pleading to the Lord about the plight of the 24 in Huizucar without a home, who were living there in exchange for picking coffee all day every day for the owner. When we were in prayer, the image of a big house appeared in my mind.

The last time we went to see María's property, we passed the house I kept seeing during my prayer times. The Lord seemed to impress on me, "There's where the children will live". I went to see the house and as I sat in the car gazing at the big old colonial house with a red-tiled roof, and noticed the numerous trees and several open areas, I began to believe what the Lord was trying to get me to believe. It seemed to be empty, so we inquired around the neighborhood for the name of the owner and how to contact him. I took the information back to our office, and talked to some of our employees about it. Some of them knew the house, and to our surprise, said it was the house of a former President of El Salvador who was exiled to Costa Rica. They had no idea how much ex-President Lemus would ask for the property, but felt it would be worth at least

$250,000. A lot more, they speculated, if the war wasn't on at that time. (President Lemus died in 1993).

I asked President Lemus to donate it to our children, but he refused. He sent word that on his behalf we were to deal with an engineer in San Salvador who was a member of his family. Having no idea about the value of Real Estate in El Salvador, I had to pray for guidance. Every time Rose Ann and I prayed about the offer we should make, $40,000 appeared in my mind. That made sense, because Bob had assured me of $50,000 and with $10,000 left over we could equip the house.

So, $40,000 it was going to be. I called Mr. Santini, and made an appointment to visit him in his office to discuss the purchase of his uncle's weekend retreat, which had one large house and a swimming pool on about three acres of land in an area with one of the best climates in the country. When I offered him $40,000 he chuckled. I was a little embarrassed, but persisted with that price. He finally advised me to put it in writing, and then he would discuss it with his family. So I did that on December 10, 1984.

My grown children, from my first marriage, together with Christopher and Teri Ann were expecting us to be in Denver for a long-planned Christmas Eve party and family get-together. It was essential that we not let them down, and so I was anxious to hear from Mr. Santini. We had non-changeable, non-cancelable airline tickets to Denver, and were scheduled to leave El Salvador at 6:00 a.m. on December 23.

Finally, on December 20, I called Mr. Santini, but was told he was on vacation and wouldn't be back in his office until January 5. "Lord", I prayed, "did I miss you?

I was sure you wanted us to have that house, and that $40,000 was the price you wanted me to offer for it." But I still somehow felt confident we were going to get it, but not in time to put the children in it for Christmas. That was disappointing, but we had to continue with our plans to leave for Denver.

We went out to the coffee farm on December 22 to tell the children goodbye and to take their Christmas gifts. Then we returned to a room we kept for our use as a bedroom in our office. We sadly began to pack.

We went out to a restaurant to eat and when we returned to our room at about 7:30 p.m., the phone was ringing. I answered it casually, but suddenly stood upright. Mr. Santini was calling to tell me that the family had decided to accept our offer, and he'd like to come see us with a contract that he had a lawyer put together. Of course, we told him how to find us. During the next hour and a half, while we were waiting for him, we finished packing for our early trip the next morning. We were happily singing and laughing.

Mr. Santini rang the doorbell at 9:00 p.m. and we showed him to our room. I read the contract, which specified an immediate cash payment of $40,000, and possession to be given January 5. I apologized to the man as I explained that we had no money right then, and had made the offer on faith that we would get it in 30 days. He actually got angry and said we were fools.

Then I assured him that we wanted to buy the property, but not on his terms. We would pay all of it in 30 days, and we had to have the key delivered to the office on December 23 so that the children would have a home by Christmas.

He was incredulous: "You mean you intend to buy that house with no investment in it and take possession of it tomorrow?"

I explained how God had spoken to me about that house, and had faith He wanted our children to live in it so they wouldn't have to move again and He would provide the money. Mr. Santini was impressed, but left shaking his head. I told him we were leaving early in the morning, and were disappointed the children couldn't have a home for Christmas, but I understood his reluctance to accept such an unusual offer. "Let the office staff here know if you can meet our terms," I said, as he reached for the handle of his car door.

At 12:30 a.m. December 23, the jangle of the telephone pierced my slumber, and I was startled awake instantly listening to Mr. Santini talking. "I have a friend who was willing to make a new contract for me at his home. I'd like to bring it over for your signature."

He arrived at 1:30 a.m. with the contract, and it was worded exactly the way we wanted it, including delivery of the key he handed me. The children took possession while we were still in the air winging our way to Denver to spend the best Christmas of our lives. Our children in El Salvador were having a great time, and we were soon to be with our family in the USA for a wonderful gathering. Isn't God good? We received the $40,000 in time to pay for the new children's home, not from Bob in Guatemala but from others.

We invited people from a government agency, the Instituto de Proteccion de Menores, to visit the new home of the children of our Shalom Children's Home, and compare it with the orphanage out in Sonsonate, and to give us permission to move those children in with our children in the new Shalom Home. In a few months they were transferred.

In Denver for the Christmas of 1984, we celebrated the birth of Jesus in several ways, a family get-together, a midnight communion service and a special Sunday Christmas extravaganza at church. After the church presentation, one of the associate pastors introduced his wife, Cheryl*, to us for the first time. Upon hearing that we were involved with a children's home in El Salvador, she told us about a lady named Judy* in Florida with whom she lived when she first gave her heart to the Lord. Being interested in any kind of children's ministry in El Salvador, we asked Cheryl for Judy's address and phone number so we could contact her.

We called Judy and asked about the home she was supporting in El Salvador. "It was in a town called Metalío," she said, "but we just sent them the money to rent a nice house on a big lake near the capital."

"Is the director's name Castillo?" I asked her.

"Yes, and the children are with him in the house on Lake Ilopango." We didn't know how to tell her what we knew about Mr. Castillo because she was so enthusiastic about her involvement with him and the children.

"We're going to El Salvador in a day or two, is there anything we can take to the children there?" I invited her to list some things, but she suggested we buy food when we get back to El Salvador and take it to them, which we did.

---

*Fictitious name to protect the person's privacy.

When we delivered the food, the children were all excited, and after they ate, we decided to pray with Mr. Castillo, a lady working there for him, and the children. Mr. Castillo asked the children to form a circle and we all held hands as I prayed and Rose Ann followed with another prayer, and one of our workers finished with another prayer.

When we broke the circle, some of the children went into a bedroom, and we could hear them crying. Our young Salvadoran worker went in after the children to comfort them while we were outside still talking to the director.

While we were in our car driving along the lakeshore on our way back to the capital, Ana spoke up, "You wouldn't believe what I learned from those older children while we were in the bedroom!" she exclaimed. "They are not orphans like Mr. Castillo said. Of the nine, seven are his. They were crying because they wanted to go back to Nicaragua to be with their mother, but he wouldn't let them. He is living with the lady who appears to work there, and has abandoned his wife in Nicaragua."

So this was another case of fraudulent behavior that the Lord revealed to us before we got too involved and spent a lot of money supporting some operation that was not ethical. We found it interesting how God always intervened and showed us whenever we were about to make a bad decision.

******

Marvin and the children were now in the new home we had contracted to buy for $40,000 (when we didn't have a dime), and we anxiously called Bob in

Guatemala to share the great news with him. We were excited to let him know that we were now realizing our mutual dream of having our own children's home together. We wanted to tell him where to send the check he promised in order to pay for starting up a new children's home.

However, he wasn't as enthused as we presumed he would be. "I've been trying to reach you by phone since before Christmas and couldn't. The people who were going to give us the $50,000 to buy a home for the orphanage are based in Holland. They agreed to finance our project, but when I told them we were finally putting the deal together for the children's home in El Salvador, they shocked me with a refusal to cooperate further because they recently verified that the U.S. government had taken the side of the El Salvadoran government to help them defeat the leftist guerrillas. Therefore, they would not send support to anyone in El Salvador, especially since I'm an American, and so are you."

Their politics got in the way of their compassion and good sense. That left me with the challenge of how God would give us $40,000 in one month. I'm not sure how it all came in, except that it was with lots of small donations, mostly from individuals. So, even though the Dutch agency wasn't faithful, our God was. He gave us another miracle, and we contracted to buy property we never would have bought otherwise.

*****

There is a beautiful, luscious, 75-acre valley that we purchased in a somewhat similar way. We had a vision to start a second children's home on a working farm. On the land we would also build a church, a hospital and a school.

I placed ads in the Salvadoran daily papers and received many offers from owners who wanted to sell their property to us so they could flee the war in their country. I went to look at most of them: some in rugged terrain and some by enticing rivers; some in hot climates and some where its cooler; some very expensive and some low priced; some that were abandoned and overgrown with weeds and some that were thriving, like a prosperous dairy farm and a large orange orchard. I tramped all over El Salvador from 1984 to 1986.

A friend of ours was a successful fund-raiser in Colorado for a large Christian agency in California. He suggested that their management invite us to explain our vision to them. After we landed in California, our good friend rented a car at the airport in Orange County, and drove me to the headquarters of the agency where we were both ushered into a large beautiful conference room. Executives from the agency ringed the large table and I was invited to take a seat in the middle.

I came prepared to explain the vision God had given us for a working farm and retreat center located on a highway that would make a church, school and hospital easily accessible to people in a surrounding rural community. This was the criterion of any land we would be interested in acquiring, though we hadn't yet found any place in El Salvador that matched our requirements.

They asked many questions about my personal character and salvation, and finally about our present projects in El Salvador. My answers seemed to be acceptable, and the men liked the photographs I passed around. The final query was about what our goals were, and that gave me the open door needed to explain about the farm we wanted to buy. I had complete books for each person, bound together with drawings of the buildings planned and the budget to accomplish the project, including the water, electrical and sewer systems. The men were pleased with the development we planned as they followed my explanations while leafing through the pages of the proposal.

When I asked them for the money to buy the property when I found it, the chief executive said: "Brother Benner you have exactly the type of project we like to invest in – agriculture, education, child care, medicine and evangelism." I felt assured that our dream was about to become a reality.

He asked the others for their assent, and it was unanimous. I left with these words implanted in my heart: "When you've found the property, arrange for its purchase and we'll send you the money, up to $100,000." As we drove on the freeway back to the airport, I sat in the passenger seat seriously contemplating all that had happened that morning. Had I heard it correctly? Was it a blank check up to $100,000?

My chauffeuring friend said, "Don, why aren't you shouting for joy? You should be rejoicing about the success of our visit."

"Well," I said, "normally I would, but I have two problems with this experience: One, big things have never come to us this easy; and two, we've had so many promises of even million dollar donations in the past that were just smoke screens, just pipe dreams. None has ever materialized, so I'll wait to celebrate about this one when I see a check that has cleared through the banks."

I set about my search again, during the war, to find the right property, and finally found it in the Department (State of) La Libertad in El Salvador. A Christian man who dabbled in real estate in that area took me to see it, and I immediately sensed that this was the land God had chosen for us.

After walking all over the 75 acres, my Christian guide made this announcement: "I'll buy this for you because if you buy it, as an American, the price will go way up; then I'll sell you the back three-fourths of the land, at the same price per acre, for your retreat center. I only want the front part, but the owner won't sell it separately."

"No way," I told him, "I need the frontage on the highway for the church, school and hospital." We separated with him vowing to look for another partner who would let him have the front piece.

A week later the man was on the telephone telling me that he couldn't sleep and was under deep conviction that he was interfering with God's plan for our ministry. It's hard for macho-oriented Latins to shed tears, but this brother was crying as he explained that if we still wanted the property, he would buy it for us. "Can you come up with a deposit of $5,000?" he asked?

"Give me 30 days, and I have faith that if this is the land God wants us to have, I'll get it." "All right," he said, "here's how I'll do it. The owner wants $100,000 for it, but I'll offer him $50,000, with $5,000 down. I believe he'll take it because you can pay in dollars, and because land is not selling very well during the war, especially in that area, and people want dollars instead of local currency so they can get to the States and leave the war behind."

On the basis of the promise I had from the California agency, I told him to go ahead. He sent me a copy of the contract so I'd have something in hand that would show the immediate need for $5,000. I called the executive in California who had been assigned our project, and he said he couldn't get the down payment for us that fast because they were in the process of rewriting our plan as a request for a grant in conformation to their standard procedures. "Go ahead and raise the five thousand and we'll refund it when we send you the full amount for the farm."

The Lord provided the down payment and we delivered it to our Christian negotiator within the 30 days allowed. The contract he wrote on January 1, 1986 specified that if we didn't have the full amount by April 1, 1986, we would forfeit the $5,000 deposit. On the other hand, if the seller decided not to sell the land at any time for $50,000 he would pay us $15,000. The contract was signed by me with confidence we wouldn't lose our deposit, and by the seller who didn't realize yet that the buyer was an American.

Then I began to telephone the California agency about every two weeks during January, and every week in February, but could get no confirmation that everything was still on "go". During a call in the last week of February, the man at the California agency made this shocking statement: "We never said we'd help you with your project. We don't know what you're talking about." It was incredulous. The Holland agency's promise to supply the funds for buying the house for our Shalom Children's Home had never materialized, and now the promise to buy this farmland for us had also vanished.

"Lord," I prayed, "You knew what I was told by those California executives, and I believe you showed us that we should buy that particular land. If they are not going to supply the funds, who is? You know that we have no money except what is donated for everyday operations of our ministry."

Here's the response I got from Heaven. "Son, if I had told you to go buy the land for the Shalom Children's Home for $40,000, I knew you wouldn't have had the faith to trust me for that amount. If I had told you to go buy this farmland for $50,000 I knew you would not have the faith to trust me for that large an amount either. That's why I let you trust in men until you had no choice but to trust in Me."

How wise is our God! How wonderful He is! How well He knows his children.

I had to trust Him for the $45,000 needed in one month to pay for the farmland for which I had signed a contract. A week later we were invited to appear on Pat Robertson's 700 Club TV program to tell about our ministry. Pat sent us round-trip airline tickets for arriving the day before we were to be interviewed on his international television program, and he put us up for the night in a five-star hotel in Virginia Beach.

The next morning we were driven to the studios with others that would be on that day's program. We were full of hope that the audience would hear our story and the money would come in for buying the farm. But it didn't work out that way. The two guests who were on the program before us were extremely interesting and entertaining. They were producing good interviews so Pat let them take more time than usual. Looking at the Studio clock, we could see that we would be fortunate if we got on that particular show.

A break came, and we heard Pat Robertson and Ben Kinchlow apologizing to their audience that they had some missionaries from El Salvador scheduled to appear but they were out of time. We were being hustled to the set as they were saying that, and so Pat said, "Well here they are now. Let's hear in the next two minutes about their ministry in war-torn El Salvador." I talked as fast as I dared, and when the floor director drew his finger across his throat to signal the end, and the cameras shut down, I felt a terrible letdown. I struggled not to show such a negative emotion, and with many apologies following us to the door, we were driven to the airport for the use of the return portion of our ticket.

"Lord, what was that all about?" I gloomily asked during the flight. "I thought sure you would use that interview to get us some money for buying the property." I didn't feel or hear any response.

A week later a check signed by Pat Robertson arrived for $25,000 to be used where needed most. We "only" needed another $20,000 and God brought it all in by April 1.

When I showed up for the closing on the sale, and the seller saw that I was an American, he balked. He said he wouldn't sell the land to us for $50,000. "That's fine," said our Christian negotiator, "Just give these Americans $15,000 and they'll look for another piece of land."

The seller suddenly realized that this was the agreement he had signed, and he didn't have $15,000, so he reluctantly signed the closing papers, and the land became ours for a tremendous bargain price.

During the ceremony when we dedicated that land to the Lord, one of our missionaries sang the hymn, "This is Holyground," and the Lord said to me, "There's the name for this farm." So we have called it Holyground which is Tierrasanta in Spanish.

After several years of trying, it became evident that we couldn't take care of so much land that extended way up the valley from the highway. The neighbors are mostly very impoverished, uneducated and unprincipled people. The majority of them were sympathetic with the leftist movement during the war and opposed to the ruling, American-supported government, and it's laws. Furthermore their perception of Americans is that they are all millionaires and if they stole anything from them, they wouldn't miss it and the Americans would soon replace it.

The neighbors didn't respect fences or property boundaries, so it became a never-ending task to police the property to keep the cutting down of our trees to a minimum; and the grazing of strange cattle, often diseased, from among ours in our grassy pastures. We had to watch so that they would not milk our cows at 4:00 a.m. before we could do it; steal our oranges in our orange grove; or rob our watermelon patch before the children in our new Shiloh Children's Home could eat them. The neighbor's pigs and goats had to be kept from entering our property through fences cut by their owners, where they ate everything we planted, etc.

So we sold several acres that were hardest to police, and received the amount we originally paid for the entire piece of land, because of the appreciation of property since the war ended, and because of the blessing of God.

We built a 12-bed hospital, a 300-seat church, a school for 100 students, and a home for the boys and one for the girls living in the Shiloh Children's Home. We raised cows, pigs, goats and rabbits through the efforts of Barbara, a dedicated, hard-working lady who came from a farm in New Jersey. She was a very wise and godly missionary, who showed the children how to tend to the animals and help with the crops. She always tied the lessons in with a spiritual theme or Bible principle, so she was not only good with the animals, but also with the children—and both the animals and the children loved her.

There was so much heat out by the Pacific Coast, where our land was located, that we couldn't raise decent crops, and the animals never did real well, either. We couldn't make a profit off the use of the land, and the neighbors interfered constantly and stole whatever they could. We couldn't find good workers in that area and it was hard to find people who would be willing to go there to work in that climate. Also, we couldn't get a telephone installed so communication was very difficult with the office in the Capital or, our other home, the Shalom Children's Home. Driving there took a long time over a dangerous road, and it soon became evident that it was expensive to employ two staffs at two Homes, so we began to think about consolidating the Shiloh and the Shalom Homes and their schools.

We started praying about how to accomplish this important change, and what we could do with the farm. I invited the Christian friend who negotiated the purchase of the farm several years before, to come take a look at the land with me, and make suggestions as to what we could do with it to make it productive. Jorge came one day, and we walked all over the property together. He was uncharacteristically quiet most of the time, and when we got back to the Shiloh Children's Home, I asked him, "Well, Jorge, what do you think?"

"Don," he said, "All the time we were walking around out there, I felt that the Lord was telling me to buy this property from you. I've been thinking about what would be a fair price to offer you for it." Jorge named what I thought was a very high price, and so we shook hands on it.

We began to see why God had us buy that land during the war when prices were low. We moved the Shiloh children in with the Shalom children, brought together the two schools, and some of the teachers and workers with the children also moved to the Shalom Home. We used all the money from the sale to improve the Shalom Home and school, building a new home for girls and another for boys, a nice church, sidewalks, playground, lots of grass, and remodeled the older buildings.

We probably would not have had the faith to sign a contract to buy an ex-president's home or a 75-acre farm in El Salvador when we had no money in the bank. It was only because we thought we had someone backing us financially that we dared to do such a thing. There are great people who could have believed God for such great things, but we weren't so strong in our faith.

Likewise, twenty years before, when we committed to go to the mission field, if God had told us then to start a mission agency, open four bookstores and establish Children's Homes in El Salvador, I wonder if we would have had the faith to do it. I'm sure it would have been too much to digest.

I'm glad that our loving Father God took us one step at a time, with a lamplight, not a searchlight, leading us on the pathway slowly, in the direction we were to take, *one step at a time*.

We praise the Lord that He is so faithful, so caring, so gentle and patient, and so forgiving.

9

CHANGED LIVES

The care of disenfranchised children in El Salvador has been a fulfilling blessing as well as a lot of work. By 1979 Rose Ann and I had our Salvadoran staff trained to handle the literature ministry without our daily involvement. That left time for us to get involved with the 3,000 children of the Christian Schools, called "Rev. Juan Bueno". Rose Ann's degree in Christian Education and her gift for teaching and guiding children into a saving knowledge of Christ made her a great fit for the school. She taught Bible classes and led chapel devotions as I helped set up the kitchens for serving lunches. We saw a great need to assist these boys and girls in other ways.

There were children following others to classes, but since many were homeless, they often missed class while looking for food. Our hearts went out to such pitiful ones, and we determined to improve their way of life. Here are some of these stories.

*****

Susana was a pretty little two-year-old, roaming a street in Sonsonate naked and crying. Her father was on drugs and her mother poisoned herself while Susana sat on her lap. She was taken in at the children's home in Sonsonate. Later as a happy and attractive teenager, Susie made two tours to the United States with our choir, and sang solos with her sweet voice.

*****

Neighbors were caring for five children because their father died and their mother was in the charity hospital dying of colon cancer. A friend of ours living in that neighborhood asked if we would take them. Two weeks after we got them settled in the Shalom Children's Home, we took them to the hospital to visit their mother, and she died at that moment, asking us to take care of her children for her as she passed into eternity. Fortunately, they got to see their mom alive one more time during that visit.

Four of these children also developed colon cancer, but we were able to save them through proper medical procedures. The oldest girl was the first person to receive surgery on her cancerous colon in El Salvador, and live.

*****

Tomas was a terrible young boy, and no wonder. He and his brother were huddling in a corner of their one-room shack when men entered one afternoon with machetes and hacked their mother to death, supposedly because her husband was a soldier who shot one of their friends during a firefight. In revenge they wanted to wipe out his entire family.

At the first blow, their mother screamed at them to run fast! They sprinted past the men who were occupied with their grisly task. They ran and ran, and eventually it got dark, and Tomas lost his little brother in the flight.

Finally, Tomas got real hungry, and started back towards his village hoping the men were gone, and he could find some food to eat. As he got nearer, he stumbled over what appeared to be a sack of oranges so he started to open it. Inside, barely discernible from the lights of the village, were the cut-up remains of his father.

In a matter of hours, poor Tomas lost his mother, father and brother. With this horrifying experience he turned out to be incorrigible. After caring for him for three years in our Shalom Home, we had to send him to a home that dealt with special needs children.

*****

Many of the children we take into the Shalom Home were abandoned by their mothers who usually fled illegally to the United States, leaving their kids to be raised by old grandmas. The grandmas have no pension and no work, and get too feeble to care for their grandchildren, so they bring them to us.

One grandma brought three children to us once because she could no longer care for them. She wanted to surrender the three and four year-old, but not the sick baby in her feeble arms. "We'll take her too," Rose Ann said. But she refused to let us have her: "she's going to die tomorrow anyway," she insisted. Because she refused to relinquish the baby, I forcibly took her away from the old woman and took her immediately to our doctor. The grandma was right; the doctor said the little one would have died the next day. She had a severe case of dysentery and hepatitis. Our doctor nursed her back to health, and "Anita" is an active robust little girl still in our Shalom Home, where her grateful grandma comes once a month to visit her and her siblings.

*****

At six years old Sara had given her heart to the Lord at a nearby church. She and her mother were living alone, and she didn't know who her father was. One day her mother allowed another man to come and live in the house with them, and he began to rape little Sara. In desperation, Sara fled from home, and when she didn't show up in Sunday School, her teacher went looking for her and found her. When the teacher heard her story, she knew she couldn't take her back to her little shack, and brought her to our Shalom Home, and told her mother where she was. Sara is now quite a little leader in the girls' section at the home, and loves to lead choruses in church.

*****

We are so used to seeing black-eyed, black-haired, brown little kids that when little Martha showed up at the Shalom Home with red hair, and a fair complexion, she became someone special. But she was so sick, and we found out why. Her father was a drunk who flew into a rage when he was drinking, and beat up Martha and her sisters, Ana, Lupe and her baby brother Moris. They finally couldn't take any more, and ran off to live in a field in hiding. Being terribly hungry, they ate grass and anything else. Unfortunately, Martha ate a lot of dirt in the field and suffered from staph infection and amoebas. She had a bad case of diarrhea and was very weak. As a result of her harsh treatment she was a mean little creature, and screamed whenever anyone tried to hold her during her first year in the home. Finally, Rose Ann was able to cuddle her, and now she is a healthy little darling who leads six other girls her age in a singing group at church services.

*****

Two little girls arrived at five years of age and had never talked. Carolina must have had a traumatic experience in her young life that affected her speech. It was over a year before we could get her to talk and at 14 years old, she is uncoordinated, has to have special-made shoes, and goes to speech classes. The other girl is Estela, who is finally able to speak intelligibly, after a year and a half of living in the Shalom Home. We have no clue as to why she couldn't talk, but praise God she is improving rapidly. Some of the other children laugh at her attempts, but Estela laughs with them because she is just naturally a happy little girl with a perpetual smile.

*****

Norma, Jaira and David were living with some neighbors who rescued them from their father who was beating them. When he tried to rape Norma, the neighbors brought them to the Shalom Home. The Christian neighbors who brought them had seven children of their own, living in a one-room shack with a dirt floor, no electricity and no water. They were very poor yet they reached out in love to these less fortunate children, and so did we.

*****

The cute mother of Tito, Elmer and Karina, had given birth to them all before she was 18 years old. Their alcoholic father ran off with another woman, and when their mother couldn't feed them any longer, she brought them to the Shalom Home. She went into prostitution and died of AIDS by the time she was 20 years old. Their father is still an alcoholic, and is not going to live much longer unless God does a miracle in his life.

*****

The father of Darwin, Daniel, Jaime and Diego was finally caught in an armed robbery and is serving many years in jail. Their mother couldn't work and take care of her four children, so she brought them to us to raise as Christians. She enrolled in a police-training course, and today she is a respected police officer.

*****

Nancy and Janet are two cute little sisters who are so friendly. They are in our care because their mother and father left them with a grandmother and grandfather. When their grandfather died, their grandmother had no way of providing for them and the evangelical pastor in that town brought them to us.

*****

Beautiful little Jocelyn has the prettiest big eyes with long lashes. She shouldn't be as happy as she is all the time; her father had already abandoned her, <u>rejection number one</u>; her teen-age mother took her to the children's hospital in San Salvador, asked a nurse to hold her while she went to the bathroom, and never returned, <u>rejection number two</u>; then the nurse took her home and tried to raise her, but after a year of juggling her duties at work with her attempts to care for Jocelyn in her home, she finally gave up and brought her to us; <u>rejection number three</u>.

*****

Yamilet, Beatriz, Liliana and Karen are sisters and are all nine months apart in age. They arrived in our care in a most deplorable condition with Karen in a cardboard box. They had parasites, suffered terribly from malnutrition and all had diaper rash so bad that their private areas and inside of their legs looked like raw red meat. Trying to apply medicine brought loud screams. Their father is a drug addict, not married to their mother who hadn't changed their diapers in weeks. She became a prostitute, but finally settled down in a humble shack with a boyfriend. When they came to visit the girls on Sunday, June 29, 1997, they attended our church service when a General of the El Salvador Army, who was a Christian, gave his testimony. The girls' mother and boyfriend accepted the Lord as their Savior, as well as others. Rose Ann had been praying for that mother's salvation for two years, so it was a special joy for her when she gave the invitation to see those two hands go up first.

*****

Diana, Dorian, Jonathan and Carlos are all very smart children. Their intelligence must be from genes inherited from their mother. Their father beat them all unmercifully, including their mother, and he finally ended up in jail. Their mother had no income, and with four little children to look after, couldn't go to work, so she brought them to us.

*****

During the war in El Salvador, a bomb exploded alongside the one-room shack out in the country, where Gonzalo, Bernardo, Marcelino, Santos and Petrona lived with their uncle and mother. Their uncle was killed while holding Gonzalo and the blast must have given Gonzalo an infirmity called hydrosephela. His head swelled up much larger than was proper for the size of his body. Their mother could only get low paying work handling a wheelbarrow for road construction. Not being able to feed four growing boys and a chubby daughter, she appealed for help. After they arrived at the Shalom Home, Gonzalo got sicker and sicker.

In those days we had insufficient donations coming in to cover the home's expenses. Prayer was the only resource we had for Gonzalo's condition, and we prayed for God to heal him and He did, but not as we expected. Franklin Graham, President of Samaritan's Purse, was in El Salvador and came to visit the Shalom Home. When he saw Gonzalo and heard his story, he immediately made arrangements through Surgeon General E. Everett Koop in Washington, to fly him to Chicago for his operation, all expenses paid. Gonzalo is now 20 years old and lives with his mother, Bernardo and Marcelino. Petrona is a mama, and Santos works in the Capital area.

*****

Julito's mother was a gang member and on drugs. She tried to kill Julito because he was too much trouble for her, and she hated him. His grandmother got him away from her and brought him to Shalom, and we gladly accepted a much malnourished, sickly little boy. His mother then tried to burn down the grandmother's house because she prevented her from killing Julito. He is a bit troublesome, but Julito is a very smart kid.

*****

Every time we drove out of the capital toward Cojutepeque, we passed a little boy sitting on the edge of the highway out in the country, with a leg that bore a gnarled clubfoot. He sat on a rock with his leg almost extended to the edge of the traffic lane. One day we decided to stop and give him some cookies and candy. He was very shy, in fact almost afraid of us. He never saw Americans close up before. A visit with him while he munched on the cookies revealed that he lived back in the bushes with his grandmother, and his name was José. He didn't know anything about his father or mother. He hesitantly led us to his house upon our insistence.

His grandmother's house was very humble, and there were nine people living in the two rooms. Most of the cooking was done outside, but they slept inside, and the visiting was done on a little porch area, where we met the grandmother. While all the others listened in as if we were in a council meeting, we asked her if she would like to see José's foot operated on so that he could walk, and run like other eight-year-olds.

The grandmother agreed to let us take José to the United States for the operation, and recuperation. It took us six months to get all the papers signed, secure a passport for José and get a visa so he could enter the U.S. An agency called "Heal the Children" found a hospital and doctor to perform the free procedure. During that time he stayed in our Shalom Children's Home and was very popular with the other children because he was a natural comedian.

We bought José new clothes, so he would look good on the airplane. When I took him to a shoe shop, he picked out a style he really liked so I bought them. Then I told the shoe clerk to keep the one shoe because he could only wear one for his normal foot. "Oh no," José said. "I want to keep that one too, so I can wear it when I come back on the airplane." His simple faith made my eyes teary. We put extra socks on the clubfoot and fixed part of a slipper on it so it wouldn't be too noticeable and not be bare.

José stayed with a family in Spokane, Washington where he was loved and well taken care of. Rose Ann and I were in Denver when it was time for José to return. After six months of operations and therapy, Heal the Children sent him to us to chaperone him back to El Salvador. We were very happy to see him, and even happier when he asked us for the other shoe. We were so glad we took it to Denver with us. José slipped it on with a big grin on his face.

When we got back to El Salvador, we went straight from the airport to the Shalom Children's Home so he could greet all his buddies there and show off his new ability to run and play with them. The children made a big "Welcome Home José" sign and it was displayed at the entrance.

I told José I would leave him there for a few days and then take him back to live with his grandmother. When I got him ready for the trip to his grandmother's house, he begged to stay at the home instead. After explaining that we promised his grandmother we would bring him back to her, and that she would want to see how his foot looks, he seemed to understand. I finally convinced him to go there by promising him that he could return to live in the Shalom Home if his grandmother approved.

José's grandmother reluctantly agreed to let us keep him if we would let him stay with her for a few days first. Afterwards José returned to his friends at the Shalom Home, and started attending school for the first time.

*****

These are the kind of children God has been bringing to us from all over El Salvador. The 250 or more children in our school, (where we subsidize their education), have similar stories. Such are the lives that we have been trying to rescue for the Kingdom of Heaven. These children have no one but us, that's why we ask people on their behalf, to send donations so that we can make a good home for them. A home where they receive nutritious food, medical care, a good education and the gospel.

Because they have a good home, our policy is to not adopt out any of our children. We are raising them to be good Christian citizens and a witness for Christ in their own country. If someone asks about adoptions we recommended that they contact a government agency to give a homeless child a decent home and a loving family, like our kids have.

While our ministry with children has been rewarding, it has also been hard at times. Especially when we don't receive enough donations to meet the needs of children who have suffered so much in their short lifetimes. Our testimony is that God has always provided, when we let people know what we need. We are speaking to others on behalf of children who can't ask for themselves. So as I look at it from that viewpoint, I don't feel guilty or embarrassed when fund raising for their benefit. "Ask and it shall be given unto you."

Therefore, if you feel inclined to be a partner in this mercy ministry, contact us at the address below. You can pledge $30 a month to our Shalom Children's Home; or if you're particularly interested in the education of unfortunate children, you can pledge $30 a month for our school; or become a sponsor of an individual child in the Shalom Children's Home.

HARVESTING IN SPANISH
AMILAT VIP 723
P.O. Box 2-5364
Miami, FL 33102-5364
E-Mail: harvest@es.com.sv
Web Site: www.harvest.org.sv

WHAT ABOUT THE FUTURE?

In earlier chapters I talked a lot about the wonderful people that God has provided to carry on our ministry. The one and most important one of all, I have left to the last. It is our daughter, Teri Ann de Dominguez. She graduated from Vanguard University in Costa Mesa, California. She provided for her education by working her way alone in California; earning money by doing Spanish interpreting for the Police Department. She also has a student loan she has paid on for many years. Teri was asked to remain on campus to teach Spanish and serve as Director of Student Ministries. She took college kids all over the world on mission trips, perfecting her Spanish while teaching. You can see that God was preparing her to work with us in El Salvador.

Finally in 1992, Teri left her well-paying, prestigious job and friends, and came to El Salvador with her sleeves rolled up, so to speak, ready to go to work. And work she does! In 1999, Teri was elected president of our mission agency incorporated in El Salvador, by the Salvadoran Board of Directors. All 6 of my living children are hard workers and are successful in their fields. One has earned a doctorate in education, and is happily employed in a school system in Missouri. Christopher is the general manager of a restaurant chain based in Minneapolis.

Teri is young and energetic; she is married to a Salvadoran Christian businessman, and has a lot of good ideas to go with her wonderful experience in missions work. Needless to say, her contribution to our ministry is invaluable and everyone connected to our mission depends on her greatly. She is fast becoming a leader in the Christian community of El Salvador. She has done wonders with our literature ministry and our four bookstores. We praise God for calling her to El Salvador to work with Harvesting in Spanish. Our Board of Directors is looking to her for the continuation of HIS now, and until the Lord returns. Rose Ann and I are looking forward to having less responsibility and stress; not retirement, but kicking back a little in the days ahead.

THE END

Christopher, Rose Ann, Don and Teri when they left Denver for Costa Rica in 1976 to study Spanish

Mr. Osvaldo Dominguez and his wife, Teri Ann Benner. He is a Salvadoran businessman, and she is President of the Harvesting In Spanish subsidiary in El Salvador, Asociacion amigos Para Latinoamerica.

The first Christian Bookstore opened by the Benners in 1977 was located in a new shopping center in San Salvador.

Max Mejia Vides and his wife, Cora celebrated their 50th wedding anniversary in January, 2000. He and Don are co-founders of Full Gospel Business Men's Fellowship International in El Salvador

Feeding the children who live on the San Salvador city dump.

The people who live on the San Salvador city dump, live in shacks like this erected from materials they scrounge from the loads brought in by the garbage trucks.

In 1986, the Benners purchased a farm in the Department (state) of La Libertad, near the beach of the Pacific Ocean, and established the Siloe Children's Home there (Shiloh Home.) In 1996 they sold the farm and moved the children to the Shalom Children's Home near the capital, San Salvador.

In 1984 the Benners purchased the home of Colonel Lemus, exiled president of El Salvador, and established the Shalom Children's Home on the 3 acres of land. Children who had no home now live in a president's house!

The campus of Girard College, Philadelphia, the orphanage Don Benner entered in 1930 and left in 1941.

Don and Rose Ann Benner with some of the children of the Shalom Children's Home, El Salvador.

These are all 70 of the beautiful children living in the Shalom Children's Home in the year 2000. Many of them are children who were transferred in 1996 from the Shiloh Childrens's Home, formerly located on the Pacific Coast.